The Drama Handbook

Teaching Acting through Scene Work

DAVINA RUBIN

GOOD YEAR BOOKS

An Imprint of Pearson Learning

Good Year Books

are available for most basic curriculum subjects, plus many enrichment areas.
For more Good Year Books, contact your local bookseller or educational dealer.
For a complete catalog with information about other Good Year Books,
please write:

Good Year Books
299 Jefferson Road
Parsippany, NJ 07054

Book and Cover Design: Nita Ybarra
Design Manager: M. Jane Heelan
Editorial Manager: Suzanne Beason
Executive Editor: Judith Adams

ISBN: 0-673-58915-3

1 2 3 4 5 6 7 8 9 10 – ML – 03 02 01 00 99

This Book Is Printed
On Recycled Paper

Acknowledgments

I want to acknowledge Gary Austin, a wonderful teacher who inspires his students to open themselves to all the gifts they have to offer.

I also want to acknowledge all my students, who are wonderful learners and teachers. This book happened because you taught me how important all the little pieces are, and how to put them together.

Table of Contents

⮾

Introduction

This handbook uses scene study to teach the craft of acting to middle-school students. A time-honored training technique, scene study focuses all the actor's available resources on one scene, rather than on an entire play. Working on a short piece gives actors an opportunity to fully explore possibilities, so that more energy may be put into the scene than in learning lines. Scene study lets a student grow beyond the basics of getting on stage and saying the lines; it enables him or her to practice the craft of acting. Most professional actors continue to take scene study classes even after they have become successful.

The book is based on two premises. First, teaching acting should not necessarily mean teaching "theater." We like to believe that teenagers in a play learn to act. Too often, however, in school plays involving adolescents, the "theater" aspect takes over, and good acting is made subordinate to "making it all work." The production becomes more important than the craft; the costumes and sets are used to cover bad performing. Since everyone has to participate, too many students end up as the "third tomato from the left" after the teacher has picked a few for the most important roles.

The second premise of this book is that teaching drama to middle-school children (grades 6–8) is different from teaching it to children of other ages. Middle-school students have grown a bit more sophisticated since elementary school. They are no longer, in their eyes at any rate, "kids." They are inhibited, but they crave a means of self-expression. The inhibition and the craving together often lock them in an internal war, battling to find a way to express themselves without risking too much in the process. Young teens can learn to use a drama class to express their own feelings and sometimes will find a new lens through which to view the world.

Why Scene Study Works

Anyone who teaches young teens will tell you that drama comes naturally to them. The trick is to get them used to being dramatic in front of an audience, whether there is a stage or not. It is an evolutionary process, throughout which one learns gradually how to feel comfortable doing things in front of an audience. A good drama class focuses on the craft of acting; it involves the skills of emotional expression, communication, interaction, movement, and cooperation. It eventually can, and often does, lead to theater work. But a class in scene work stands on its own as a valuable educational tool.

Once students are beyond elementary school, the idea of playing a small part in a class production holds less appeal than ever. On the other hand, pre- and early adolescents are not always ready for the broad scope of a full-scale production. Many middle schools do not have the facilities to stage such productions, and many middle-school teachers, unless trained in the dramatic arts, lack the skills to truly teach students the craft of acting. The idea of a large production can be as intimidating to a teacher as it can be to students.

Scene work, therefore, makes the ideal heart of a middle-school drama program. It offers students the opportunity to pick the work they want to do, to choose their partners, and to make decisions about the presentation of their scenes. It gives them a chance to be a "star" in an unthreatening setting. It also gives them a degree of control and practice at decision making, both integral to any education. Scene study allows students to explore a wide range of expression, both emotionally and intellectually, as actors, writers, and directors. On a personal level, this often affords them an insightful look into their own and others' behaviors.

When students tackle small acting tasks in front of a group and are successful at them, they are willing to attempt more. The more they succeed, the more they are willing to try. Eventually, instead of feeling a fear of failure, they look at performing as something at which they can succeed. Unlike a large play, scenes do not loom as huge performances, but rather as "works in progress," with which students can study, re-do, and experiment.

Teachers assigned to do a drama class can also be caught up in the fear of inadequacy and failure, especially those with limited experience in dramatic productions. Because scene study focuses on teaching a craft, not on creating a production, you will find that once started, the program practically runs itself.

Setting the Stage

∽

Before students begin their scene studies, there is some preliminary work to do. Begin your drama classes with group activities that build trust and at the same time help you learn about your students. These are nonthreatening activities, so students usually have fun and leave class with a different attitude about the word *drama*. It is important for them to understand the relevance of trust to a drama class. On stage, they must be able to trust that the other actors will be there for them.

These exercises can take from three to five class periods, depending upon how many students you have, how often you meet, and the length of your class period. The exercises have great value, as they enable students to examine and define their emotions. If you take longer to do the exercises do not panic. Taking time with these will yield results later.

Trust Circle

Though I learned this activity in Gary Austin's improvisation workshops, I have been in many other classes which also do trust activities similar to this. If you know others and feel comfortable with them, use them as well.

Have students stand in a circle. You stand in the middle of the circle and ask a student to come into the center. The student stands in front of you and closes his or her eyes. Gently turn the student a few times, making certain that you hold on so that the student is not dizzy when he or she starts walking. When you let go, the student, eyes still closed, must walk back and forth across the circle. Students in the circle stop the walker by gently placing their hands on each shoulder, and then gently turning him or her around and letting go. The student then walks across the circle again, and continues to do this until you say to stop. Students standing in the circle must be as quiet as possible.

Find a place for yourself in the circle after the student begins walking. This enables you to watch the students and model for them what you want done.

When you first explain this exercise, tell the students what you will want them to do when their turn is called. First demonstrate with your eyes open, and, as you walk back and forth, tell students they will have their eyes closed. Then close your eyes and keep walking.

You will notice that many students flinch long before they get to the edge of the circle. It's as if they have suddenly walked into a wall; tell them to walk through it. This teaches them to trust the people in the circle, but, just as important, to trust themselves and their own judgment. They know there is no wall there, so they should keep walking.

WHAT STUDENTS LEARN ◆ The Trust Circle teaches students to trust each other and to be trustworthy. This is of major importance for actors on stage who must trust all the others they work with. When one person trusts another, it gives both people more confidence. Talk to students about the trust necessary to do a scene with another person.

WHAT YOU LEARN ◆ You will see the dynamics of the class and how the students interact. The Trust Circle will teach you a great deal about students' personalities and responsibility levels, and how well they cooperate. You will spot the students who need attention, those who are more fearful or shy, and those who are not able to take on the responsibility you have asked of them. All this comes, not from watching the child in the center, but from watching the children in the circle.

Count to Ten

Improvisation teachers use this exercise. I have seen several variations of it, such as Running the Alphabet. Count to Ten works better for large classes. Use this activity within the first few days of a drama class and during the term as well.

> Have students sit in a circle and tell them they are going to count to ten. Explain that because the counting will be random, no one will know who is going to say each number. If two or more people say the same number, you must start over from the beginning. Generally, it's a good idea for you to start off the first few times and let the class continue. At some point, simply sit in the circle and leave it up

to someone else to start. At times students
will not hear the two voices say the same number,
so you must listen carefully and be the arbitrator.
If the students "get away with" reaching ten
without actually following the rules, they are
never really happy.

This is a fascinating exercise to watch. It can take anywhere
from a few minutes to an hour, and you will see the class go
through many emotional changes. First, students will giggle
and laugh when two people say the same number. After a
while, they will get exasperated, then they will start
targeting those students who *always* have to say a number,
and often say two or three. As they get closer to ten, they
will groan and laugh when they fail. Then they will regroup
and begin again.

Some students will call out every other number; others will
always say the same number. Some students will try to
control it all by "assigning" people numbers to call out.
A bit of gentle coaching is sometimes necessary, but try to
limit it. If students do the exercise on their own, it makes
their achievement that much more satisfying. As you coach,
point out why it is necessary to be silent sometimes. This
is another trust activity. Students must learn to trust that
someone will eventually say the next number.

Finally, they will reach ten. There will be cheering and
clapping, and they will feel like a team.

WHAT STUDENTS LEARN ♦ Count to Ten takes teamwork, cooperation, patience, and participation. Students learn that sometimes not talking is as valuable a contribution as talking. One interesting aspect of this exercise is that "cheating" gives no satisfaction. I have seen a class do this by keeping scrupulously to the rules, because winning only meant something if the students really did it.

WHAT YOU LEARN ♦ This exercise offers another chance to see the group dynamics in action. You will notice your shy students, who never call out a number at all. (You might coax: "I want someone who has not called a number to start us off with number one this time.") You will also identify the students who need to control by orchestrating the whole activity and telling other students which number to call. You will observe the students who must say a number and are almost compulsive about it.

Five-Second Look

When my students filled out their last journal entries for drama, I asked them which exercise had helped them the most. A surprising number wrote Five-Second Look. I say surprisingly because I designed this exercise for teaching public speaking and communication, not acting.

This exercise helps speakers overcome a fear of being in front of a room of people. Students learn to scan an audience, giving equal eye contact to all parts of the room. Though not really an acting exercise, students say it helps them to be more comfortable on stage.

PART ONE: From the front of the room a student must look at a member of the audience (class) for five seconds without looking away. Then the student shifts the gaze to another class member and does it again. The student must do this five times.

You should sit in the audience and keep track for the student by counting, "1, 2, 3, 4, 5 change, 1, 2, 3, 4, 5 change," and so on. If you see the student's eyes flick away from the person, start the count at one all over again.

PART TWO: After the student looks at five people for five seconds each, he or she stands in front of the room, and scans the audience, looking up and down each row, making eye contact with each and every person in the room.

PART THREE: Give the students a sentence. The student must say the sentence, scanning the room at the same time.

You can make up sentences on the spot, or in advance, if you feel more comfortable doing that. (Some examples: "It is amazing how healthy you can be with a good breakfast." "Unfortunately, some people do not know how to fill out an application for a job.") These sentences should not be long and should not have much emotional content.

WHAT STUDENTS LEARN ♦ Students have a chance to see how easy it is to talk in front of a group and look professional. Emphasize that someone in the front of the room feels that everyone in the audience is looking at him or her. But, the fact is, the person in front of the room is looking at the audience, too. If you are in front of the room, and you look at someone for more than a couple of seconds, that person will either look away, or will *work* at looking at you. Most people will look away. Make sure you stress that in front of the audience, *you* are in control of whom you look at and how long you look.

WHAT YOU LEARN ◆ Watch how students in the audience react. You will learn something about their levels of cooperation and trust from this exercise. Watch the eye patterns of the students as they do this exercise. Those who cannot seem to hold a look for five seconds are often very fearful; their eyes will flicker everywhere. Don't give these students parts that are very difficult or long right away.

Emotional Inventory

For this exercise, group students in groups of three to five. Talk a little bit as a class about the fact that every emotion looks a little different. Not all people cry when they are sad or laugh when they are happy.

Begin by giving the students an emotion to examine. The groups have two tasks:

1. *Tell what the emotion looks like. This means describe that emotion's observable behaviors. For example, what does sadness look like?*

Students might describe heavy sighs, deep breaths, looking down, slumped posture, eyes not sparkly, a frown or turned down mouth, possibly teary or not focused eyes, slow movement.

2. *Tell what would or could cause a person to feel the emotion. Students might list death or loss, moving, parents' divorce, lost pet, or not getting something expected as causes of sadness.*

Here is a sampling of emotions to choose from:

- Happy, anticipating, cheerful, excited, enthusiastic, ecstatic, giddy, enchanted
- Sad, bitter, depressed, disturbed, disillusioned, disappointed, forlorn, morose
- Angry, bitter, mean, furious, violent, annoyed, frustrated, sadistic, irritated, cranky
- Rude, obnoxious, contemptuous, scornful, cold, abusive, snide
- Pleased, content, fulfilled, satisfied, delighted, smug
- Interested, fascinated, intent, curious, thoughtful, nosy
- Scared, terrified, hysterical, lonely, embarrassed, needy
- Shy, timid, nervous, cowardly, ashamed, defensive
- Worried, concerned, anxious, overwrought
- Sneaky, sly, vengeful, cowardly, vicious, jealous
- Generous, kind, sincere, loving, fond, affectionate, sensitive

- Devilish, rowdy, rambunctious, boisterous, lively, naughty, evil
- Mysterious, aloof, withdrawn, apathetic, unfeeling
- Brave, pugnacious, bullying, antagonistic

Do this with five to seven emotions during a class period. When students are working on a scene, have them look at the specific emotions of their character and do an inventory for emotional behaviors to use.

WHAT STUDENTS LEARN ◆ This is a good time to introduce the more subtle emotions and to define and explain what they are. Students know *happiness* and *sadness*, but often don't think as much about the shades of emotions, such as *cranky, annoyed, bitter*, or *furious*. Have students examine the facial and body aspects of an emotion. This allows them to think about what *they* do when they are experiencing these emotions, and gives them a variety of behaviors to help them show a character's emotion on stage. It also can help students more clearly define and get in touch with their own emotions so that they see they are not always angry or sad; they might simply be cranky or disappointed.

WHAT YOU LEARN ◆ When you give students awareness and control over their emotions and how they are expressed, you are providing a great gift. This can also help in dealing with problem students who don't perceive their emotions clearly when they are in the middle of acting them out.

Emotional Alphabet

Here's another activity that explores the expression of emotion.

> Have students sit in a circle as you give a scenario for the emotion you want. For example, "Your child has just walked in the door at 2:30 in the morning, no explanation, no apology. You are very angry."
>
> You then say the letter "A" with this emotion. The next student in the circle says "B" with the same angry emotion. Give each student a chance to express that emotion, using only letters of the alphabet. Then pick another emotion: nervous, very happy (won the lottery), sad (grief), interested, and so on.

Some students won't do this. They will say every letter the same way. Don't push too hard at this point. If you let them be, they will feel more relaxed after a while, and they will apply this when the time comes for them to do something on stage. Alternate which direction the alphabet is said, so the same person isn't always first.

WHAT STUDENTS LEARN ◆ This and the other emotional exercises help students to see the subtleties of emotional expression and how much control they can exert over emotions. By taking students outside of emotions, these exercises help them understand better what creates emotional reactions. These exercises also give students a beginning repertoire of emotions that they can expand as their acting experience grows. Also, as students come to understand emotions, they come to understand themselves better.

WHAT YOU LEARN ◆ The Emotional Alphabet will immediately show you the students who are extremely shy and those who are willing to take risks. Though students should choose their own partners for scene work, it helps to encourage a shy person to work with one who is not.

Emotional Attendance

For this exercise, you'll need to create a set of cards illustrated with faces showing different emotions. Write the emotion under each face and laminate the cards. Alternatively, simply make cards with different emotions written on them.

As students enter the room, hand each one a card. Before you take attendance, ask students if there is anyone who does not understand the emotion on his or her card. Clarify any terms they do not understand.

Explain that you are going to call the attendance and each student must answer with the emotion he or she has been given. At times you can have an extended conversation, if you wish.

Teacher:	John Jones
John:	Whadayou want?

Teacher:	I'm just calling attendance, to see if you're here.
John:	You can see me cantcha?
Teacher:	Are you angry about something? (If you're right, student says yes.)

WHAT STUDENTS LEARN ♦ This should be a fairly quick exercise. You may find that during the quarter students often ask to do it again. They learn many different emotions, which will help them later in their acting. This exercise also helps students to recognize when they are feeling antagonistic, or angry, or frustrated, and it enables them to explain how they feel more easily.

WHAT YOU LEARN ♦ By this point you should know which students will respond easily and which ones might still be too shy to do more than respond to their names.

Some Theater Basics: Words and Movement

∞

Now that you have laid the groundwork for the class, the next step is to teach students some basic terminology and skills that will help them in doing their scenes. Don't clutter their minds with vocabulary; teach enough so that they know the proper stage terms and understand that acting is not just walking on a stage and saying lines. Don't test students on these terms. Just explain them when necessary and have students apply the knowledge in class. You may have to reiterate the terms but students will learn them eventually simply by having to use them.

Stage Geography

Students should become aware of the terms that describe locations on the stage. All directions for stage performance refer to the actor's point of view as they stand on the stage facing the audience. *Stage right* means the side of the stage to the actor's right; *stage left* is to the actor's left. *Downstage* is that part of the stage nearest the audience. If directions call for a character to move downstage, they move toward the audience. *Upstage* indicates that part of the stage away from the audience, toward the back. One of the most important things to remember is not to put an actor in the position of being *upstaged*. This happens when he or she has to turn to face another actor who is upstage. The actor turning upstage will have his or her back to the audience, who will then miss facial expressions and even words that the actor speaks.

The *fourth wall* is the imaginary wall between actors and audience. It is not *really* there, but for the purpose of the play, actors must put a wall there, so that when they are performing, they never acknowledge that someone is watching.

The whole point of acting is that, when actors are on stage, that is where they live. People come to the theater to watch them act out their lives on the stage. If an actor lets people know that he or she is aware of their presence, the performance is ruined for them. It is no longer real; by acknowledging the audience's presence, the actor says, "This isn't real, it's just a play, and we know you're watching."

Another way of breaking the fourth wall is by *breaking character*. This means an actor stops being a character and becomes himself or herself on stage. Reminding a fellow actor of lines, or whispering or giggling on stage are all ways to break character. Making eye contact with the audience is another.

A major acting rule is: **Don't break the fourth wall**. An actor should never look at the audience to let them know he or she is aware of their presence. This cardinal rule holds true through the end of the scene. Sometimes students finish a scene and then look at the teacher or the audience as if to say, "We're done." They don't do that in real life, so they shouldn't do it on stage. They should simply continue the action until the lights are turned off *(blackout)*, or you give some verbal cue that the scene is finished.

Of course, as with all rules, there are exceptions. If the playwright or the director so directs, an actor may break the fourth wall. For example, in Shakespeare, the *aside* is a sentence or two spoken directly to the audience. The actor does this on purpose because the author has written his play with instructions to do so. Some monologues also require direct contact with the audience. However, even when directed to look at the audience, an actor never breaks character.

THE WORLD'S A STAGE

You do not need a stage to teach drama. My classroom was originally a room for fourth graders. The counters were low, with a sink set into the middle of one counter. So I put wallpaper on the bulletin board above the counter with the sink in it, added "curtains" to hide a nonexistent window, and then proceeded to use that as the kitchen of a house. Kids could study at a table, set a table while talking, watch television while sitting in the kitchen, talk on the phone, or wash the dishes. Finally, some students and another teacher built a set of six-inch high platforms that serve as a stage in my room. But we got along for a couple of years without it. Over a period of time furniture and other props appeared, and eventually the sets began to look like those of a small theater.

Stage Movement

Movement on the stage is known as *blocking*. Where the actors go when they say their lines, where they stand, and where they enter from are all part of the blocking. When a director tells an actor to "cross to stage left while saying a line," that is part of the blocking. A director will often refer to notes in the margin of his or her script about blocking, such as "X to door, stage right" (*X* means "crosses"). Blocking is very important in a play. Without good blocking, the actors look as if they are just standing around talking. Blocking should be as natural as possible and should not be used just to move actors around.

Entrances and *exits*, when actors arrive on stage and leave, are both part of blocking, as is some of the *stage business*. Stage business refers to the activities an actor does, either to establish aspects of the character (twirling hair or biting nails to indicate nervousness, for example), or simply as part of the scene's necessary actions, such as opening a refrigerator and getting out a soda, or rummaging through a purse looking for makeup.

Props is short for *properties,* anything that is put on the stage to be used in the play or is brought on the stage to be used by the actors. Tables, chairs, telephones, lamps, an ironing board, a book of matches, all can be considered props if they are needed in the play. A door is not a prop because it is part of the stage set. But if the actors carry a door onto the stage during the action, it would be considered a prop. Larger props that are a part of the stage set but are not picked up by the actors are called *set props*.

Once the acting exercises and scenes get started, appoint two or three students as the *prop crew*. These students are responsible for finding out what is needed for the scene and getting it set up. If you are doing exercises such as entrances or exits, tell the prop crew what to put on the stage. If a scene is being done, the actors should consult with the prop crew who set up the stage according to their wishes.

This gives responsibility to the students in two ways. First the prop crew must be responsible for setting up and breaking down, or *striking*, the set. But it also places the responsibility for the stage set on the actors in the scene. This means they must think about their blocking, their stage directions, and their props before they perform the scene.

Stage Behavior

Several important terms refer to the acting itself. When an actor is *off book*, he or she knows all the lines and no longer needs the script. The actor might stumble occasionally during rehearsal, but for the most part does not need the script. *Projection* means using the proper voice methods to be heard by everyone in the audience, and a *beat* is a tiny pause just before an actor delivers a line.

Improvisation is acting without a script and can be very helpful for a variety of reasons. Actors often improvise scenes between their characters to get a feel for how they might behave in different situations. An ability to improvise can also be useful just in case something unexpected happens during a scene. If an actor forgets a line or misses an entrance, being able to improvise provides a way to cover up problems without alerting the audience that something is wrong.

Motivation is the reason a character has for doing or saying something. An actor who moves out of the way as another actor comes on stage needs to know why the character is moving. It's not "to get out of the way of the other actor," but rather "when she comes in my character knows there's going to be a problem and doesn't want anything to do with it." Or it might be as simple as "I was really tired and wanted to sit down."

THE "I DON'T WANT TO DO THIS!" STUDENT

In my first year of teaching this program, a student in one of my classes loudly announced that she was not going to do any of the exercises. I simply said, with a big and sincere smile, "no problem." She was very tall, much taller than all her peers, and a class leader. I was not going to put her through the humiliation of trying to be stopped by a circle of "little people" in the Trust Circle. But neither was I going to let her start a stampede of "Idawannas." I made no fuss over it, not even to say "I understand," or question her after class. At the end of the quarter she came up and asked me if she could do the Trust Circle. Though we were way beyond that point in the curriculum, for this student it was the perfect time. Her request also told the class that she now trusted them.

The Reluctant Actor

Every once in a while a student will tell you that he or she does not want to do a particular exercise. Make *nothing* of it in front of the class. Just a "no problem" or "your choice" very quietly will make that person safe, but remove the power the student's choice has over other students. If the student chooses to do nothing for a particular exercise, then he or she will fail that exercise. When one student advised me she would not do a scene, I told her that she had a choice but that doing nothing would earn her a failing grade. Then, when all the other students had chosen their scenes, I said, "Lynn since you're not doing a scene, I want you to make yourself useful. Listen to the scene Carla and Shannon are doing. Help them learn their lines and tell them if they sound realistic." She became a "director," and, yes, she did come and ask me if she could participate when students chose their second scenes. Once students begin to rehearse and practice, the activity is contagious.

As an "Exploratory Arts" teacher, I taught all three grades (6–8) in my middle school. The class was not an elective; I saw every student in the school. Sometimes students walked in the first day and told me they would rather take an F than get up and make fools of themselves. I am proud and happy to say that quite a few of these same students are now acting in small theaters, and some are already involved in fledgling professional careers. A few have told me "It's all your fault! You've created a monster." So do not be discouraged by students who are not interested in drama. Most of them are just nervous, and, when they realize that they do not have to perform in a play in front of the school, they usually settle down. The format presented here is one which appeals to almost every student I have taught.

Basic Acting Exercises

The exercises that follow will help students learn the basics of stage movement, speaking to an audience, and using props.

Entrances

Every entrance is also an exit. When a person enters one place, he or she leaves another. When you teach students how to enter, make it clear to them that they will have to think of where they have come from before they enter. The purpose of this exercise is to get students to show emotion when they go on stage, so that the audience recognizes their feelings and wonders what is happening. This is the first "acting" that students will do. Use the door to your classroom, unless you have an actual stage to work on.

It is helpful to tape and show to the class a variety of entrances from different television shows, preferably shows with which students may not be familiar. That way, they can focus on their learning without having to make a lot of comments about a familiar show or personality.

> Give each student a situation, something that happened before the entrance. This situation will determine what emotion the student will enter with, and how the student will behave. Here are a few suggestions:

1. *Two bullies from school threatened you on the bus and followed you. You finally broke into a run and got home. Now that you are home, you might check to see if they are still out there. (Student could enter in a frenzy, out of breath, hide, check windows, etc.)*

2. *The boy (girl) you like just asked you to go to the movies on Saturday. You are ecstatic.*

3. *At the end of your last-period class the teacher told you she is failing you because you did not hand in all your work. You handed in everything, but she will not even listen. You are furious. (Student could kick door, throw backpack across room, mutter, etc.)*

4. *Your friend told you to meet him at his house. You knock, walk in, call out. No one is there.*

5. *You must sneak into a house to get back something that belongs to you. If the police come by, it will look like burglary, so you have to be very careful.*

6. *You hear the phone ringing as you are trying to get your key in the door. Hurry! (A variation of this is to have two students race into the room, both trying to get to the ringing phone, grabbing the phone away from one another.)*

7. *It is a very hot day. You come home to a cool, air-conditioned house. What a relief!*

8. *You are a new student at a school. You come into an empty room and sit, waiting for the teacher and the class to show up. You are nervous.*

9. *Your mom called you to tell you your pet poodle, Fluffy, was hit by a car. You enter your house, and, by habit, you expect to see Fluffy run toward you. Then you remember.*

10. *Your little brother and dad just drove off to the movies. You were all prepared to go, but your dad said you couldn't go because you didn't finish your homework, and he sent you back in the house to get it done. You may be angry or unhappy. Use your books as props.*

11. *You have just learned that you were chosen to be on the all-star team, which means a trip to Los Angeles and Disneyland. You come home to tell your parents.*

12. *You are really worried; your mom has been sick for a few days and has been in bed. She doesn't even pick you up from school. This is something that has never happened before.*

Try making up your own situations. Put them on laminated colored cards so that students can pick from a variety of situations. Or, you can simply give them a situation, or let them make one up, once they get the idea. It's okay if students do an entrance that's been done already. Occasionally a student will pick a situation you know he or she isn't ready for. Give him or her another. If students are uncertain about what to do, coach them or give them suggestions.

WHAT STUDENTS LEARN ♦ Students find out that coming on stage is an acting task on its own. They begin to understand the idea that you don't just "show up" on a stage and wait until it's time to say your lines. You are acting as soon as you enter the stage area. They learn that this is fun!

WHAT YOU LEARN ♦ It is great fun to watch this exercise. Students who volunteer first usually ham it up (and sometimes overdo) and have all sorts of ideas about how to do a particular entrance. After a while, other students will start to think of ways that they would have done a particular entrance, and they will volunteer. Every student does an entrance. If a student has a particularly hard time, have another student help, so that it is a two-person entrance. Students who volunteer to help will often have an idea and will make the exercise easy for the other student.

Though it rarely happens, don't let students get away with just walking in the room and standing around. Gently but firmly get them to see what is needed for the entrance, so that when they do it, the applause and praise received are worth it.

Silent Actions

Here's a way of teaching students about stage business. It's called Silent Action because students are not required to speak during these activities, but they quickly get the idea of being on stage and doing something besides just standing or sitting. The purpose of the exercise is to get students to be so comfortable on stage that they are no longer thinking about the audience. Often, if a student gets totally engrossed in figuring out math problems, or threading a needle, he or she will not be concerned with who is watching. You might also assign students a situation or mood level to go along with the activity, such as frustration or boredom.

Have students conduct the following stage business at the front of the classroom, or devise your own activities to have them try.

- setting a table

- clearing a table

- doing math problems

- writing a letter to someone

- eating chips and watching TV (trying to convey what is being watched to the audience)

- sewing—threading a needle, etc.

- ironing

- dialing a phone, getting a busy signal, waiting, dialing again

- looking for something that must be found (e.g., tickets to a game or concert)

- listening to someone on the other end of a phone, unable to get a word in (expressing frustration, anger, interest, or boredom)

- fixing something

- hammering nails into something
- sanding a piece of wood
- measuring something (a table, liquid, fabric, a wall or window, another person)
- writing spelling words ten times each
- looking up words in the dictionary and writing definitions
- cutting out snowflakes or patterns
- cutting out pictures from a magazine for a collage
- trying on clothes
- putting things in size order
- putting cards in order (all hearts, diamonds, or all aces, twos, threes, etc.)
- playing solitaire
- exercising, lifting weights
- making a sandwich
- doing nails
- putting on makeup
- combing hair, making a braid (the student's own or someone else's)
- waiting anxiously for someone
- reading a book
- hiding something

Once in a while, try having another student go up while one student is doing a silent action, and they then can improvise a scene. For example, a student is sewing something. A second student comes in and asks "What're you doing?" A short scene can take place while the student *continues* to do the activity.

In all cases, students are to use props, and really do the activity. For example, if setting a table is the stage business, then make dishes and utensils available.

WHAT STUDENTS LEARN ♦ Students learn that actions are a necessary part of acting. Students also learn that speaking is not always the most important behavior one performs on stage. An actor who is simply reading a VCR manual can gain an audience's attention without saying a word.

WHAT YOU LEARN ♦ You will come to recognize the point at which the student stops being self-conscious, and begins to focus on the exercise. This will eventually help you to be a better coach.

Exits

The purpose of this exercise is to teach students how to leave a stage and not just walk off. Students learn to act until the moment that they are out of sight of the audience, so that there is no break in their character, or in the emotions on stage.

For this exercise, have students begin on stage. They should act out a particular emotion while they are on stage. They then make an active decision to leave the stage. This decision should be based on something, not just a "get up and walk out" motion. Some ideas are listed below, but you and your students can make up many others.

1. *You are reading a newspaper and suddenly notice something in the paper that excites/upsets/ overjoys/angers you. (You can tell the student what he or she sees.) You read for a moment or two, then get rid of the paper in an appropriate manner (throwing it down, crumpling it, throwing it in the air with a whoop of joy, etc.) Exit in an appropriate fashion to fit the emotion.*

2. *You are on the phone talking and/or listening. You finally put down/slam down/gently lay down the receiver and exit in an appropriate fashion to fit the emotion set up by the scene.*

3. *You are watching TV or reading. You hear something. You leave the room in a mood that indicates whether the sound is something to fear, or something to trigger a surprise welcome, or something that elicits anger toward a person arriving.*

4. *You enter the room, see something, back away, and run out. It might be anything from a dead body to a note reminding you of an important date.*

5. *You see something outside, go out to help, investigate, get something, and so on.*

Have several students do the same exit with different emotions.

WHAT STUDENTS LEARN ◆ Students learn that an exit isn't just "walking off," but is a part of the action, and is motivated by something. They learn to keep in character until they are off stage and out of sight of the audience.

WHAT YOU LEARN ◆ You will see how quickly students drop out of character. You can help them by suggesting that they decide what they (as the character) will do once they have left the stage.

Vocal Exercise

This exercise is a short one, designed to show students the best way for breathing to project their voices.

> If you have a room with carpeting, have students lie down on the floor. If there is no carpeting, students can bring towels for this exercise. As they lie on the floor, ask them to put their hands on their stomachs. As they breathe, have them "fill up" with air, and note the rise and fall of their hands.

This simple exercise helps students to see how to breathe properly to project their voices so that they can be heard by everyone. It is important that students learn how to breathe properly (even when standing up!) so they are able to use their lung power to its fullest capacity.

Blocking

Good blocking is essential to the success of a scene.

> Have a student go up on stage and sit on a chair or couch. When you say "move" the student moves to another area while talking. He or she may say anything, as long as there is talking of some sort taking place. If the student finds it especially difficult to think of something to say, make something up on the spot. ("So, you think Eileen will go out with you after this?" "How was I supposed to know you got suspended?" "You know if Mom finds out, you're a dead person.") When the student reaches another spot on stage, he or she finds something to do, or just sits, or leans, or stands.

WHAT STUDENTS LEARN ◆ It may feel strange at first to do nothing but move from place to place reciting nonsense sentences, but it gives students the feel for moving on a stage while talking and helps them later incorporate blocking into their staging.

Using Props

Students love to use props. Use a small closet or bookshelf in your room for storage and send a letter home to parents requesting that they not throw out the "dead" microwave or an old iron. Parents and students can donate old clothes, small vases, even couches and lamps. Make sure you send a letter of thanks to anyone who is generous enough to send you things. It sounds like a small thing, but it should not be forgotten.

Food as a Prop

Students love to eat, but when it comes to eating on stage, they often get shy and inhibited. For example, if given a potato chip to eat while doing a scene, many students will hold the chip for the entire scene. What does the audience watch? The potato chip! To train your students to eat on stage, use little bags of chips, cookies, or pretzels. Get them to eat these with a partner while doing homework, playing cards, or just watching television in front of the class. They should talk and act normally.

As an assignment, tell them to watch people during lunch to see how they talk while eating food, or to eat a bag of chips while studying with a friend.

WHAT STUDENTS LEARN ♦ Once students master the technique of eating on stage, they will find it can be a natural part of their stage business. They will learn how to talk with a small amount of food in their mouths and how to use the eating as part of the acting.

Introducing the Scenes

❀

Once students complete the basic exercises, they are ready to begin scene work. Read through or describe the available scenes for the students. The first group of scenes they do should be short (some *very* short). After you read them, have the students pick their scenes and their partners and rehearse using the method explained below. Make certain that you give them a deadline for learning their lines and deciding how they will act out the scene. Then set aside several days for performances. Have students sign up for rehearsal time for on stage and for scene performance dates.

Learning Lines and Rehearsing

Before learning lines, students should do several things. First, they should read through the script a few times to make sure they understand it. Remind them to look up any words they don't know, or ask you to explain them.

When students have read through the script enough to have an understanding of the lines, they should read through it again and block out the scene as they go. Remind them to write down the directions they have chosen on the script so that they will remember their blocking when they rehearse.

If you have a large class of students, all of whom are doing scenes, you can portion off sections of the room, send some students into the hall, and accommodate them as much as possible so they will have separate places in which to rehearse their scenes.

Students have the responsibility of deciding on their entrances, stage business, and props. Some scenes do not require an entrance from offstage; students may be on stage at the start. Their first scenes will require very little blocking, as they are quite short, but as the scenes get longer, the requirements for all other aspects of the scene become more complex.

All students should sign up for a time to work on the stage or performance area, just to see how the scene works out. This should be only a short period of time, enough to read through the scene and make any corrections or changes in blocking.

One of the most difficult things for new actors to do is to learn lines. However, reading through a part several times gives the student a general grasp of the lines, so that when the time comes to nail them down, he or she has a pretty good start.

If two people are learning a short scene, tell them to learn six lines at a time, three for each character. They should do the lines four, five, six times, until they can do them without reading them. After they feel confident with these lines, they go on to the next six. When they have learned those six lines, they add on the first six, and work on the twelve lines until they have learned them all. Students continue to do this until they know the whole script. As students progress in acting, they start to learn bigger chunks, sometimes as many as a page or two at a time. But to start, always have them learn little pieces at a time. If they get stuck on a particular section, have them do it over and over and over and over, until they know it well.

Be warned, students will ignore this aspect of learning if you let them. They will learn the first six lines, then they will start reading through the rest of the scene. Then they will go back, read the first six lines, and then read the rest of the scene. After a full class period, they will know only the first six lines. *Insist* that they learn the scene in small chunks, little by little. Demonstrate it with a student. Pick a short scene and read the first six lines aloud about five to seven times. Then you and the student put your scripts away and say the lines. You'll find that not only do *you* know the lines; the whole class will know the lines. Students can learn a whole script this way very easily. Then they are not dependent on scripts and can rehearse the scene, including blocking and stage business, without a script.

Some students have trouble reading or memorizing from reading. But if they hear the words, they can memorize. For these students, either tape the scene yourself, or have a student do it. A *very* successful method is to tape the scene through once, then re-tape only the other person's lines, with spaces left on the tape during which the student can respond. Using this tape, the student can rehearse any time, because the scene partner's lines are on tape.

After the Lines Are Learned

It's not enough to know the lines. The words have to mean something. They have to have life, emotion. After the students know the lines, have them practice saying the lines in different tones, until they think the lines sound like real people talking. Slower readers might need help with this, but after they have read a line several times, it will start to make sense, and they will have more of an idea of how it should sound. Teacher coaching is very helpful at this point. Some students might like to coach (direct) as well. Use discretion and your knowledge of your students here.

ACTING CAN BE FUN

*The assistant principal of my school sent a visitor—
a friend who had decided to become a teacher—to
observe my classes. We were in the rehearsal phase
of our class. I took attendance, spoke to the class
briefly about learning lines before blocking too
much, and then told them to go to their appointed
rehearsal areas.*

*Most of the students left for the hall or the area
outside my room. The young man watched,
obviously surprised and puzzled.*

>   *"Where are they going?" he asked me.*
>   *"To rehearse," I said.*
>   *"Won't they run away?"*

*His remark made me laugh out loud. The picture of
all my students running away struck me as very
funny. "No," I said, "go and watch them. They
enjoy this."*

*He came back about a half-hour later, amazed at
how self-motivated the students were. It really isn't
so surprising, though. After all, they had picked
their scene partners, picked the scenes they wanted
to, and were in charge of the whole "production."
They had a strong investment in the outcome of
their performance.*

Performing the Scene

Students should set up the performance area with the help of the prop crew. They may bring in their own props, or you may provide them.

Have one person be the *prompter*. This person reads along as the scene is being performed and is prepared to help if a student forgets a line. If an actor forgets a line, he or she should simply say "line." This is the signal to the prompter to give the actor the next line. When the actor says "line" there is no break in the action and *no break in the fourth wall*. Of course, the best scenario is that the other performers cover for each other, so the missed line is not even noticed, but as this is a performance workshop setting, and the students are not professionals, it helps them to know that if they forget a line, someone will help.

Remind students that it breaks character and the fourth wall if they start to give scene partners their lines, or look at them in anger. Once on stage, that is where the actor lives. If an actor forgets lines in the scene, the others should wait for him or her to say "line," or else cover up by improvising.

Remind students before they perform their scenes that at the end of the scene they should go back to their activities, or make up lines, or exit, but they *must not break the fourth wall*. One easy way to end the scene is to assign someone to turn off the lights after the last line is spoken. This allows the students to end the scene and not feel the need to improvise until you tell them to stop.

Notes and Critique

When students do their scenes for the first time, it is helpful if you take notes as you watch. Let the students do the scene through once with the idea that they will get a chance to do it again. Note what they have done well and also how they could improve the scene. Note especially their line delivery and blocking, but also take into account their body language, use of props, stage business, and emotions.

Make sure that your notes are always geared to making the performance better and to identifying what is good about the performance. Always address the students as actors, fellow workers who are trying to produce something.

Let students know that their scenes are works in progress, and that it is customary for an acting instructor to discuss the good and the bad together so that improvement can be made the next time the scene is done. Students get to re-do their scenes, unless the first time through is so wonderful that you feel they are ready for more challenging roles.

After the scene is over, tell students about the notes you have made. Share your notes with each student in front of the class. Listening to critiques helps the other students as well. Such comments as, "I'd like to see you get more angry," or "Try slamming the book down when you say you're angry, and let's see what that looks like," are very helpful.

Remember, every scene is a learning exercise for the whole class, so critiques should all be designed for experimentation and improvement. If you feel the scene needs little or no improvement, don't try to find something. Give the students a big win on their scene. The next one they do might be longer and more difficult and will provide more challenging learning experiences as well.

Here are other scenarios where your constructive criticisms should be made.

> Gary has just done a short scene in which he is supposed to be angry, but he never really lets the anger fly.

> **Teacher:** Gary, let's try something here. When you say, "I'm not going and that's final!", what if you threw something? You could throw the magazine you're reading. Let's see what that looks like. (If this does not work, you can get ideas from Gary, his scene partner, or the class.)

> Marissa did a scene with two other girls. She kept getting upstaged, so the audience neither saw her face, nor heard her.

> **Teacher:** All of you go and stand where you were when Tammy called Marissa a little gossip. (Students take their places.) Okay, if Marissa stays there, she has to turn her back to the audience to talk to Tammy. How can we work it so that Marissa is not upstaged? (This gives all the girls the opportunity to work out the problem of blocking.)

> Two boys just did a scene in which the entrance took a long time, but did not add to the scene. It gave the boys little time to actually be on stage.

Teacher: Y'know, I'd like you to try something. What would happen if you were to start the scene on stage? No entrance. What kind of stage business could you do?

In all these situations, you should leave the door open for students to self-correct.

In some instances, you will find that the students just are not at a level of awareness or sophistication about stage work where they can figure out what to do. When this occurs, you should still make suggestions with the idea that these are only suggestions. This is a work in progress; therefore, one can make adjustments.

Try to make as many positive comments as you honestly can; always have at least one positive comment, even if it is "I know how shy you are, and I am so proud of you for actually getting up and doing a scene." A key word in critiquing is honesty. Do not tell students that they are wonderful actors if they did a poor job. It makes fools of them and makes praise for truly gifted actors worth nothing. Avoid comments that will make students feel uncomfortable. Comments like "Jennifer, you didn't even try up there" are a no-no. If you have a student who seems particularly unsuited for the acting task, try to find one that would be more appropriate for him or her.

Grading Students' Work

〜∞〜

It is not an easy task to grade students' work in an area as subjective as acting. However, you must bear in mind that you are not only grading the performance of the students on stage; you are also grading the performance of the student in your class. For this reason, you should take several areas under consideration as part of your grade:

Count each of the short exercises done in class. I grade on participation and enthusiasm, as well as performance. Therefore, if a student does an entrance that is exceptionally good, he or she might get an A. If another does an entrance with a lot of shyness and nervousness, but, after a few trials, really does a good job, he or she would also get an A. My feeling is that any student who has shown a willingness to participate (which should include all of them) should get at least the equivalent of a C for the opening exercises.

Students get a grade for rehearsal. Walk around to monitor what students are doing to learn lines, block out the scene, and so on. You will easily see the degree to which students are applying what they have learned.

Give students an audience grade. Actors should be the best audience, as they understand more than most how difficult it is to get on a stage and perform. It is important for students to learn the proper behavior for being a member of an audience. Give students a grade for their overall contribution as a member of the audience.

Grading the performance. This is not as tough as it seems. Some performances will be wonderful. The students understand the dialogue, they use all the right moves, and they are impressive. These are the easiest to grade.

For those performances which are not as obviously stellar, you can further break up the presentation into component parts. This can be done on a small chart, on which you can put a score for each element. Grade students on use of expression and emotion in dialogue, blocking, natural movement/stage business, vocal quality, and consistency of character. This last has to do with keeping in character even when the character has no lines, or is making an entrance or exiting the stage.

Give students credit for knowing all the lines—sometimes, at first, that is all a student might achieve, and if he or she has worked hard at that, a small success will lead to greater risks in later performances.

There are some students who might not do as well the first time out, but when you give your suggestions, students who follow these and actually improve should be given a great deal of credit. Students who get up and do the performance, have learned the lines, and have made an obvious effort to do it right deserve at least a C for their beginning efforts.

Name of Student: _____

Overall Grade: _____

Character: _____

Expression/Emotion _____

Blocking _____

Stage Business _____

Vocal Quality _____

Character Consistency _____

Lines Learned _____

Comments _____

_____

Name of Student: _____

Overall Grade: _____

Character: _____

Expression/Emotion _____

Blocking _____

Stage Business _____

Vocal Quality _____

Character Consistency _____

Lines Learned _____

Comments _____

_____

You should consider giving grades for some or all of these:

Group Exercise (give a small value to each exercise)

Entrance

Silent Action

Exit

Scene 1—rehearsal

Scene 1—performance

Audience

Scene 2—rehearsal

Scene 2—performance

Audience

For the second scenes, you can be a bit more exacting for grading purposes. Students by this time should know what they need to do to produce a good scene, and they should be held more accountable.

Act on It!

❦

You now have several useful tools for running a successful classroom drama program. With the following short scenes written for students you can "break the ice" in your classroom. Some of the scenes are very short and can be learned easily in a class period. Use these for your more timid students, or for students who have a hard time reading and/or memorizing.

Read the scenes to your students so they are familiar with them and can make wise choices for their first performances. This might take a class period or two, but it is well worth the time spent.

Let the students pick their own partners and scenes. This will get a real buy-in from them. (If you see a potentially bad combination in your class, tell them beforehand that they may not work together.)

After students have done one short scene you may give them the opportunity to perform a longer, more complex scene or monologue. Several excellent books are available from which students can choose. For their second scenes, students must work with a new partner. This will ensure that they will get a variety of acting experiences with different people.

As a final note, be aware that although the names in the scenes indicate male or female roles, in many cases the names can be changed. Often, scenes can be performed by two girls, two boys, or a boy and a girl.

Short Scenes

Test Time

Scary Movie

Food for Thought

Beauty is Only Skin Deep

Part of the Family

My Mom Doesn't Love Me

Just a Joke

Ball Game

Help!

Best Friends

Thief

Stolen Diary

Have You Heard?

Read Between the Lines

Clean Up Your Act

If It Feels Good

Test Time

Erin: Did you study for Mr. Cheng's test?

Shayla: Study? I practically inhaled the pages. Three chapters of history crammed into my brain.

Erin: Did you take notes?

Shayla: Erin, you know I always take notes. I can't study any other way.

Erin: Can I borrow them?

Shayla: What for? The test is next period; you'd never be able to read them all anyway.

Erin: Never mind.

Shayla: What's going on?

Erin: I didn't study. I'll probably flunk.

Shayla: Stop being melodramatic. You never fail anything. Remember Mr. Heifetz's math midterm?

Erin: That was different.

Shayla: You cried and told everyone you failed because you left out all the last problems. Then it turned out everyone left out more than you, and you got the highest grade. So don't talk about failing, okay?

Erin: This is different. I didn't study. I'm definitely going to fail.

Shayla: So, what did you need my notes for? They won't help you now.

Erin: I could keep them on the floor.

Shayla: What? Cheat? Get off it, Erin. You've never cheated in your life.

Erin: Always a first time.

Shayla: Erin, you are the only person I know who would truly lose respect for yourself if you cheated. Don't even think about it. (*Watching* Erin) What's going on? What's wrong?

Erin: (*Visibly upset*) What am I going to do? I've never failed a test before.

Shayla: How come you didn't study?

Erin: My dad is sick. We were at the hospital all last night, and I just didn't have time.

Shayla: Erin, why didn't you tell me?

Erin: I don't want to talk about it. It's too scary.

Shayla: Tell Mr. Cheng. He'll let you take a makeup test.

Erin: I don't want someone to give me a makeup test because he feels sorry for me. I hate kids who do that.

Shayla: That's because you know most of them are full of it. But this is legitimate. Get your mom to write a note.

Erin: I don't want to use my dad as an excuse. It makes me feel worse.

Shayla: Maybe you should just go home. Call your mom and go to the hospital to be with your dad. I'll tell Mr. Cheng where you are. Just go. Do it!

Erin: I don't know . . .

Shayla: Erin, go home. Your mom probably needs you. Stop worrying about a lousy test. No one will care but you.
(Erin *hesitates*)

Shayla: Erin, go home.
(Erin *exits*)

Scary Movie

Bill: I really want to see the Freddie movie marathon.

Bob: Not me. They're so gory, and I get really scared.

Bill: You get scared? Like, for real?

Bob: Yeah. I have nightmares, and my mom won't let me go anymore.

Bill: That's weird.

Bob: Oh, right. You mean to tell me you don't ever get scared when you see those kinds of movies?

Bill: Well, in the movie I do, but once it's over, I don't think about it any more.

Bob: You just go home and forget it?

Bill: Yeah. (*Pauses, thinks*) Well, I remember having nightmares after one movie I saw when I was little.

Bob: Which one?

Bill: I think it was . . . (*Thinks for a moment.*) *Bambi*. Or *Dumbo*.

Bob: (*Laughs*) Oh great! You think I'm weird because I get scared by a mass murderer, and you got scared by *Bambi*!? Give me a break!

Bill: Well, I was really young.

Bob: How young?

Bill: Oh . . . seven.

Bob: (*Laughs*) Seven? Scared of Bambi? Give me a break!

Bill: (Bill *continues to defend himself, and* Bob *keeps teasing, as the lights go out.*)

Food for Thought

Scott: Hey, Kev, you want to come over to my house? We could order a pizza and play video games.

Kevin: Nah. I'm trying to keep my weight down so I can make the freshman wrestling team next year.

Scott: You don't need to worry about your weight. You never change.

Kevin: I don't worry about it. I just don't eat everything in sight.

Scott: Well, then don't eat pizza. You can just watch me eat pizza. Hey, you're not getting one of those weird eating diseases, are you. Like anorxia?

Kevin: It's anorexia. And no, I do not have anorexia. With anorexia people don't eat at all. I eat.

Scott: Yeah, but what's one little pizza?

Kevin: One little pizza is enough to keep me off the wrestling team in my weight class. Besides, I don't need a pizza. There are people starving out there, and I don't need a pizza.

Scott: How did we jump from the wrestling team to starving people?

Kevin: Well, it just seems that everywhere you look people are obsessed with food. There are ads all the time for food on every channel, in every magazine. And there are kids whose only decent meal may be the school lunch. I mean, how do they feel watching television and seeing families eating huge meals, when they don't have anything?

Scott:　Whoa! You're going a little fast for me. First you say you don't want to eat because of the wrestling team. Now you say you don't want to eat because other people don't have a lot of food. What's going on?

Kevin:　Nothing is going on. I'm just trying to say there's a difference between *needing* food and wanting to eat just to stuff your face. I mean, my brother comes home every day from school saying he's starving. He doesn't even know what starving is. I just want to eat when it's meal time, or when I really feel a need to eat. Like, if I get thirsty, my body *needs* water. There's a difference between that and someone who says, "I'm dying of thirst."

Scott:　Kev, those are just expressions. People don't really mean them.

Kevin:　Yeah, but think what it sounds like to someone who really is starving, or dying of thirst. You asked before if I had anorexia. Now there is the stupidest, most selfish disease there is. I mean, someone decides they need to look thin, and they starve themselves for looks, while all over the world people look like that because they are starving. It makes no sense.

Scott: Where is all this coming from? All I asked is if you wanted to come over to my house for a pizza and some video games. I didn't think we were going to get into a deep philosophical discussion about world problems.

Kevin: Sorry. It's just been on my mind lately. I think there are kids at our school who really don't get enough to eat. It makes me feel bad. I mean, you don't really have to eat a pizza, do you? What if we took the money and spent it on food for a local food bank.

Scott: You're kidding, right? Why don't we just buy sandwiches and give them out to homeless people?

Kevin: That's a great idea!

Scott: Kevin, you are getting a little weird, you know that? I mean, I like you and all, but you are getting strange.

Kevin: Just because I'm thinking about other people does not mean I'm strange.

Scott: How about if we compromise? I'll make a sandwich at my house, *and* we can put five dollars in the supermarket "feed the needy" box.

Kevin: Would you do that?

Scott: Anything, just to get you to shut up and be a little normal again.

Beauty Is Only Skin Deep

Melissa: I really like Marty Lincoln.

Brianna: Well, I don't.

Melissa: It doesn't matter if you do or not, you're not the one who's going out with him.

Brianna: Thank God for small favors. Look, I really think it's my duty to warn you. I don't want my best friend going out with a dork.

Melissa: He is not a dork. He's just a little different.

Brianna: A little? A *little different?* Mel, the guy dresses like a Sixties hippie, he doesn't drink soda because of the caffeine, and he reads all the time. And let us not forget his—uh—size.

Melissa: Okay, so he is a little chubby. But that's not the point.

Brianna: Well, what *is* the point?

Melissa: The point is that he is really nice, he respects me, and he has a brain. I can talk to him, and he treats me as if I'm smart. He listens. It's what's inside that counts, and he's got a lot inside.

Brianna: But the guy is fat and ugly.

Melissa: Hey, I happen to like him. A lot. And I don't appreciate you talking about someone I like. I wouldn't let anyone talk about you that way.

Brianna: Okay, I'm done. I have said my piece. But I still think it's a mistake.

Melissa: Time will tell. Just remember that some of the most successful men in America were once nerds.

Part of the Family

At start of scene, Matt *is obviously very upset.*

Ken: Hi.

Matt: (*Does not respond*)

Ken: Earth to Matt. Helloo? Matt, what's wrong? How come you've been out of school?

Matt: My dog died.

Ken: Your dog died? No wonder you feel bad. What happened?

Matt: She was just old, that's all.

Ken: Well, you can get another dog, can't you?

Matt: Not like Sasha.

Ken: Well, she wasn't exactly a person, Matt. I mean, I think you're exaggerating just a little.

Matt: Do you have a pet?

Ken: No. My mom doesn't like mess in the house, and pets always make a mess. My brother has a goldfish.

Matt: Well, then you wouldn't understand. Sasha's been my friend ever since I was a little kid. She was the first thing I saw when I woke up, and the last person I spoke to before I fell asleep. She was part of the family.

Ken: Matt, she was a *dog*, not a person. You can hardly say a dog is a member of the family.

Matt:	Oh really? Tell that to my parents. Sasha saved my little sister's life when she was a baby.
Ken:	I'm sure she was wonderful, and I can understand why you're upset, but you act like it's the end of the world or something. I mean, I just don't get it.
Matt:	Remember when your grandmother died last year? How would you have liked it if someone said, "Well, really Ken, it's no big deal. She didn't even live near you."
Ken:	That's different. She was a person. A relative. And I loved her.
Matt:	Yes, but you only saw her a few times a year. And the last time she came to visit, you were upset because it meant you couldn't go camping with us. So what's the big deal?
Ken:	She was a *person*, Matt. A member of our family. Not a pet.
Matt:	Well, you could always find some other old woman to take her place.
Ken:	What? That is a really mean thing to say.
Matt:	I'm not being mean. I'm just trying to make a point. Sasha was a part of our family, and I could no more replace her with another dog than you could replace your grandmother with another old woman.

Ken: I cannot see how you could compare losing my grandmother to losing your dog.

Matt: There's no use talking about this any more, because you just don't understand.
(*Exits*)

Ken: My God, it was just a dog.

My Mom Doesn't Love Me

Marco:	I hate my mother.
Tony:	C'mon, you don't really mean that. She's your mother.
Marco:	Why does everyone say that? Why is it everyone assumes that if a person is a mother, she must be a good person?
Tony:	I didn't say that. It's just that everyone loves their mother.
Marco:	Well, I don't. I mean, why should I love her if she doesn't love me?
Tony:	Of course she loves you.
Marco:	There you go again. "Of course she loves you." My mother doesn't love me. She doesn't love anyone but her work. She's never home for anything. So why do you just assume that she loves me, or that I should love her? She's not really a mother—she just lives in the house.
Tony:	Why does she work so much?
Marco:	She loves work.
Tony:	That's ridiculous. Nobody loves to work so much that they wouldn't come home to be with their kids if they could.
Marco:	Well, my mom does. She sometimes doesn't

come home until ten o'clock. Then she eats cold supper, or says she's eaten, and watches the news and goes to bed.

Tony: It doesn't sound like the ideal life to me. Do you think she stays out late to party?

Marco: Party? My mom? She wouldn't know how. She's exhausted every night. She's always worrying about some thing or other. She's too uptight to party.

Tony: She doesn't sound too happy to me. I mean, if she's so awful, why is she working so hard, instead of just doing what she wants?

Marco: How do I know? Ever since my dad died, you'd think we were dead, too. Sometimes she acts as if we're not even there. My brother and I might as well be orphans.

Tony: Have you ever talked to her about it? I mean, have you ever asked her why she works so hard?

Marco: Yeah. She said something like, "I'm doing it for you." That's a laugh.

Tony: Why are you such a brat? Can't you tell that she's working so you can have nice things and live in a nice house? She's working hard so you can have a normal life, go to college and all.

Marco: Yeah, well, she could work less and spend more time with us.

Tony:	Why don't you tell her that?
Marco:	If I ever saw her, I could.
Tony:	Wait up for her tonight. Tell her she doesn't have to work so hard. Why don't you offer to help, instead of being such a selfish little baby?
Marco:	Will you knock it off? You sound like some psychologist.
Tony:	No, I just think your mom is working so hard to give you the things you're used to, and you're too self-centered to see it. How many hours do you think she had to work just so you could go on the Great America trip?
Marco:	I don't know. Just drop it, okay?
Tony:	No. You brought it up. You said you hated your mother. Most kids would love a mother who worked so hard so they could have nice things. You want your mommy home, and you want nice things. Well, face it. You mom has to work to make a lot of money to keep you and your brother happy. And you work at making her unhappy.
Marco:	I never thought of that.
Tony:	Yeah, well, start thinking.
Marco:	I am. I think I'll take the bus home and start dinner.

Just a Joke

Mika *enters, ignoring* Lisa, *going about her business. She might slam something down, or push something* of Lisa's *aside.*

Lisa: You don't have to act mad at me. I said I was sorry.

Mika: Well, sorry isn't good enough. I'm sick of your stupid jokes.

Lisa: You have to admit, it was a little funny.

Mika: Oh yeah? Well, I'd like to know how you'd feel if someone did that to you, in front of someone *you* liked.

Lisa: It wasn't so bad.

Mika: It was awful. He'll never speak to me again.

Lisa: Sure he will. I'll talk to him myself.

Mika: Don't you dare. He'll think it's another one of your tricks.

Lisa: (*Sincerely*) I really am sorry. Really I am.

Mika: How could you do this to me? *Why* did you do it?

Lisa: I don't know. I thought it would be funny. We always used to play tricks on each other, and now that we're in the same school again, I just figured. . .

Mika: Well, you figured wrong. This isn't fifth grade. I'm not a little kid any more, and I did not appreciate your spraying whipped cream all over me in front of Eric.

Lisa: I'm sorry. I really didn't think you'd be so upset.

Mika: Well, at least now I know where all the whipped cream went.

Lisa: I had it hidden under my bed in the little cooler. I was nervous last night when you couldn't find any for the ice cream.

Mika: You were nervous, but Mom was mad! She still doesn't know. (*Pause*) Of course, I *could* tell her.

Lisa: Oh, c'mon, you wouldn't. Would you?

Mika: I won't if you let me wear your green shirt.

Lisa: That's new! *I* haven't even worn it yet.

Mika: Well, it's that, or I tell Mom.

Lisa: Okay, okay. But don't get it dirty, okay?

Mika: Okay. Unless, of course, someone gets whipped cream on it.

Lisa: Very funny.

Ball Game

Jose: Did you see the game last night?

Miguel: Yeah. It was kinda pathetic.

Jose: Well, I think if a team has three people out injured, it makes a lot of difference in how they'll play.

Miguel: Yeah, but 57 to 3? What kind of score is that?

Jose: They'll get better.

Miguel: They'd better. If they don't, they'll never make the playoffs.

Jose: I don't think they will this year. But they've been in the playoffs for years. Let someone else get in there.

Miguel: No way! I bet on their games, and I want them to win.

Jose: You bet on their games? Are you crazy? Where do you get the money?

Miguel: From my dad. I get a pretty big allowance. He thinks it makes up for the divorce, and his being away so much.

Jose: Does he know you use the money to bet?

Miguel: Nope, and he won't, 'cause I win a lot.

Jose: You could get into a lot of trouble.

Miguel: If I do, maybe my dad will have to pay more attention to me.
(*Return to activity, talk about it as scene closes.*)

Help!

Tyrone:	I need help.
Daniel:	Yeah, I know. You need help with your hair, your face . . .
Tyrone:	Very funny. I really need help and you're doing a comedy routine.
Daniel:	What's up?
Tyrone:	Some guy in my class is threatening to beat me up.
Daniel:	How come?
Tyrone:	What do you mean, "How come?" What difference does it make? He wants to grind my face into hamburger.
Daniel:	Well, he must have a reason. People don't just wake up one morning and think, "Wow, I know what I can do today. I'll bash Tyrone's face in."
Tyrone:	Will you stop being so cute and help me out here?
Daniel:	What do you expect me to do? Beat him up?
Tyrone:	No, but . . .
Daniel:	But what? And while we're at it, why is the guy planning to beat you up?
Tyrone:	I told you, it's not important. He just is, that's all.

Daniel:	If you can't trust me to know what's going on, I can't help you.
Tyrone:	I stole something of his.
Daniel:	What! You stole something? You stole something of his, and you don't know why he's going to beat you up?
Tyrone:	I didn't say I didn't know why. I just didn't say why. And it isn't exactly a "something." It's more like a . . . "someone."
Daniel:	You stole a someone? A person? You stole a person. How do you steal a person?
Tyrone:	She's his girlfriend.
Daniel:	Uh-oh. This could be bad.
Tyrone:	It is bad. I just told you. He wants to beat me up.
Daniel:	*Who* does?
Tyrone:	Frank Riley.
Daniel:	You're kidding, right? It's a joke.
Tyrone:	No, I'm serious. And scared.
Daniel:	I don't blame you.
Tyrone:	So, what are we gonna do?
Daniel:	We? Where do you get a "we" outta this?
Tyrone:	You've gotta help me. I'm desperate.
Daniel:	No, you're crazy, especially if you think I'd risk my life for you over Frank Riley.

Tyrone: What's the big deal?

Daniel: The big deal is he weighs 220 and could lift me over his head and throw me to Kansas. Forget it.

Tyrone: He'd never do that.

Daniel: Well, I'm not waiting around to find out. You got yourself into this, you get yourself out. (*Exits*)

Tyrone: My life is a mess.

Best Friends

Jackie *is seated at a table, reading, or doing homework, when* Ann *enters.*

Ann: Hi.

Jackie: Don't "hi" me!

Ann: What's your problem?

Jackie: *I* don't have a problem.

Ann: Yeah right.

Jackie: You're the one with the problem.

Ann: Excuse me?

Jackie: You heard me.

Ann: What is going on? What did I do?

Jackie: I don't want to talk about it.

Ann: (*Grabbing* Jackie's *book*) Jackie! Stop it! Talk to me.

Jackie: (*Pulls her book back*) Why don't you go talk to a wall or something. Or, better still, why don't you go talk Melissa?

Ann: Melissa? Why would I want to talk to Melissa?

Jackie: Because Melissa is your new best friend. The one you think is nicer than anyone.

Ann: What? Who said that?

Jackie:	You did.
Ann:	When? When did I say that? (*Pause . . .*) C'mon. Tell me when I'm supposed to have said that. You never heard me say that.
Jackie:	No, but Nissa and Charlene did.
Ann:	That's a lie. Those two are just itching to start a fight between us, ever since you got the concert tickets.
Jackie:	Oh, right, blame it on them.
Ann:	I'm not *blaming* anyone, I'm just telling it like it is. I was eating lunch with Melissa yesterday because you were taking your make-up test. Those two lovely friends of yours came over and asked where you were.
Jackie:	And what did you say?
Ann:	I told them you were busy, and I was busy eating lunch. So then Nissa says, "Oh, you've found a replacement for Jackie. Isn't it nice to have a new little friend?"
Jackie:	Then what?
Ann:	So I said, "Well, she's nicer than anyone I see around here."
Jackie:	You didn't tell them she was nicer than me?
Ann:	No. But it sounds just like Charlene to say something like that. She's always trying to start trouble.

Jackie: And what about Melissa?

Ann: She's really nice, J. You'd like her. And she can't wait to meet you.

Jackie: (*A bit suspicious*) How come?

Ann: Because I told her all about you.

Jackie: How come?

Ann: Because *you're* my best friend.

Jackie: (*Big smile*) Yeah. Hey—maybe Melissa can use the third ticket to the concert.

Ann: Maybe. Now, would you move over and let us get some work done?

Thief

As Jason *enters,* Chris *is counting out a roll of bills.*

Jason: Hey, Chris, how'd you get so much money? You never carry that much around.

Chris: You promise not to tell?

Jason: Yeah, I guess so.

Chris: Good. I got it from the teacher's desk.

Jason: You stole it?

Chris: Not exactly. It was on the floor right by her chair. I saw it fall out when she opened the drawer.

Jason: (*Louder*) That's stealing!

Chris: Will you shut up! I should never have told you.

Jason: Why'd you do it?

Chris: I wanted it.

Jason: Yeah, but it's not like you're poor or something. Besides, I want lots of things, that doesn't mean I just take them.

Chris: Well good for you. Anyway, I'm gonna pay it back. So it's just borrowing.

Jason: How much did you take, anyway?

Chris: I *found* forty-five dollars.

Jason:	What if she finds out? That's not just a few bucks.
Chris:	You won't tell. You promised.
Jason:	So when are you going to pay it back?
Chris:	Whenever I get a chance. Stop being so pushy.
Jason:	I'm just worried, that's all.
Chris:	Why be concerned? It's my life, not yours.
Jason:	Yeah, but I like Mrs. Rowe. I don't think it's fair you took her money. It's not like she makes as much as your dad. (Mrs. Rowe *enters, obviously distressed.*)
Mrs. Rowe:	Hey, guys, I've got a problem. Did either of you find some cash lying on the floor in my room? I must've dropped it, but I've backtracked from my car to here and it's gone. (Jason *looks at* Chris *to see if he will tell.*)
Chris:	Uh, yeah. I was just telling Jason about it.
Mrs. Rowe:	Oh, thank heaven! I was really worried about it. I have to fill up my car with gas, and that's the last of my cash.
Chris:	Here it is. It's all there.
Mrs. Rowe:	You deserve a reward for being so honest.
Chris:	No, that's okay, Mrs. Rowe. My dad would be upset if I accepted anything. I'm just glad I could help.

Mrs. Rowe: Well, thank you so much. I'll see you
              tomorrow.
              (*She exits*)

Jason: That was pretty good. She didn't guess a
              thing.

Chris: Yeah. I guess. Let's get outta here.

Jason: Hey, Chris?

Chris: 'Sup?

Jason: Did you really need the money for
              something?

Chris: (*Beat*) Nah. If I want something, I can always
              work for it. That's what my dad says I have
              to do from now on. I guess it's not so bad.
              (*Beat*) Hey, Jas?

Jason: Yeah?

Chris: Would you have told?

Jason: I don't know. I'm glad I didn't have to think
              about it.

Chris: Yeah.
              (*They exit as they speak the last few lines.*)

Stolen Diary

Lisa *and* Nick *enter from outside, arguing. Each has a backpack slung over a shoulder.*

Lisa: I cannot believe you! I am never speaking to you again.

Nick: Oh, like that's gonna be a big loss.

Lisa: Shut up. Don't even speak to me.

Nick: Do you notice me speaking to you?

Lisa: You just wait 'til Mom comes home.

Nick: Hey! We had a no-tattling agreement.

Lisa: Well, I'm breaking it. This is too mean and awful for you to get away with.

Nick: I didn't do it to be mean. It was just . . . I don't even see what the big deal is.

Lisa: You don't. You don't. What do you think it is? You steal my diary and you read it out loud on a bus full of loudmouth dweebs, and you think that's funny? That diary is my personal stuff. MY thoughts. MY feelings.

Nick: Yeah, your feelings about Kevin, Jared, Steve, and half the boys in the class.

Lisa: (*Beginning to cry*) I hate you! You've made my life a misery.

Nick: Oh, come off it! First of all, I did not steal your diary. You put it in my backpack by

	mistake last night. And second, I didn't read all of it. I just read the important stuff about Jared.
Lisa:	Yeah, with Jared and everyone else listening. You should've used the bus driver's microphone, they couldn't hear you all the way in the back.
Nick:	Well, I was really just reading it for Jared. I can't help it if my voice came out so loud.
Lisa:	Why would you do something so mean? Why would you read something like that to a boy I really, really like? You purposely humiliated me and made me a laughing stock in front of him.
Nick:	If you ask me, he's the one who should be embarrassed. I mean, the guy is shy, y'know. And then he finds out that you have all these ideas about him.
Lisa:	Yeah, well he wouldn't have found out if you hadn't read it to him.
Nick:	Well, he asked.
Lisa:	He asked what? He came to you and said, "Oh, by the way, if you ever get hold of Lisa's diary, I'd really like to have you read it out loud on the bus."
Nick:	No. NO! He asked if you ever asked about him. I told him no, but that I saw something about him in your diary. I wouldn't let him have it, which is why I read it to him.

Lisa: Jared asked about me? You're just making this up to cover yourself.

Nick: I swear, he did.

Lisa: So, uh, what did he say after you read that part to him?

Nick: He asked me for my phone number.

Lisa: Why didn't he ask you for my number?

Nick: It's the same number, you twit.

Lisa: Is he going to call me?

Nick: I guess. Are you going to tell Mom what I did?

Lisa: If he calls me, I won't.

Nick: But he might not call right away.

Lisa: I'll give it three days. But if he hasn't called by Thursday, you are a dead brother.

Nick: He'll call. (*Smiles*) Take my word for it.

Lisa: How can you be so certain? What are you not telling me? C'mon, talk, you little twerp.

Nick: I have said quite enough. I promised Jared I wouldn't say anything. You're supposed to be surprised when he calls.

Lisa: Ohmygod! This is FABulous! I am . . . ooooh! Where's my diary? I have to write this all down right now.

Nick: Diary? You want your diary? (*Holds it in the air, waving it around*)

Lisa: Nick Stoneman, you give me that diary NOW, or you will not have a head. (*Chases him out of the room, both blabbing, but they are both smiling*).

Have You Heard?

Sarah: So, Denise, how come you and Jan hate each other so much?

Denise: We don't hate each other. She's just jealous of me, and I don't like to be around jealous people.

Sarah: That's what she said about you. That you're jealous and spiteful.

Denise: She's just saying that because she claims I started a rumor about her, so now she wants to get back at me.

Sarah: What rumor?

Denise: Nothing. Forget it. It was just a little joke, that's all. About her and some guy. She got all upset over it.

Sarah: Didn't you used to be best friends?

Denise: Yeah, until she stole a guy I liked.

Sarah: Was he your boyfriend?

Denise: No, I just liked him, and I told her how I felt about him. But he started liking her, and she went out with him anyway.

Sarah: Well, it sounds as if you're the one who got jealous. So you made up a story about her and acted as if it was true?

Denise: Yeah. She deserved it.

Sarah: Just like I deserved it because Derrick spoke to me at lunch yesterday?

Denise: You were with Derrick yesterday?

Sarah: Yes, as you well know. But I wasn't *with* him, I just talked to him while you were at the Pep Club meeting. But I'm sure you heard all about it and decided to start something about us, too.

Denise: Us? What do you mean, "us"?

Sarah: Oh, c'mon Denise, don't play dumb. I know you started talking about me and Derrick.

Denise: No, I didn't. Honest. I didn't even know you were with Derrick. And I didn't start a rumor about you.

Sarah: So *you* say. Do you really think that's the way to keep a guy?

Denise: Derrick? I like Derrick, but not that way. We're friends. I'm happy if you like each other. Honest—I didn't start any rumors.

Sarah: Oh, really? I don't believe you. You're the only one who would stoop so low.

Denise: No, lots of people start rumors.

Sarah: That's where you're wrong. Lots of people don't start rumors or talk about someone just to be mean. And the ones who do eventually have no friends. Like you. It's a lucky thing Jan told me about what you were saying, before it got around the whole school.

Denise: Hey, wait. I didn't say anything. Honest.
I swear.

Sarah: Oh? Then who did? Jan, I suppose. Jan
started a rumor that you started a rumor.
Forget it, I don't want to be around you any
more. You're no friend.
(*Exits*)

Read Between the Lines

Jared: Hey, Thomas, c'mere a second.

Thomas: What do you want, Jared?

Jared: I need you to read something for me. I can't make out the handwriting.

Thomas: What is it.

Jared: A note from that new girl.

Thomas: Who, Tenisha?

Jared: Yeah. She wrote me three notes so far this week.

Thomas: New Honor Society student is writing you letters? Mr. "school is for nerds" himself? Does she know who she's writing to?

Jared: Yeah. She just probably finds me irresistible.

Thomas: What'd she say?

Jared: Here, I got them in my backpack. You can read them.

Thomas: Hey man, I don't want to read letters you got from some girl.

Jared: No, it's okay. Go ahead. Read them.

Thomas: (*Begins to read the first letter*) Hey, this is a little personal.

Jared: It is? I mean, you think so?

Thomas: (*Reading from letter*) "Every time I see you I feel funny—like my world is turning upside down. I want to spend some time with you, get to know you better." You don't think that's personal?

Jared: Well, yeah. I didn't read that part yet.

Thomas: It's the first sentence.

Jared: I didn't read them yet.

Thomas: Then what are you giving them to me to read for?

Jared: No reason. I thought you might be interested, that's all. I wanted to hear how the words sound, you know, like someone talking. Makes more sense to me that way.

Thomas: (*Starting to realize* Jared *has a problem reading*) Right. So, which one did you get first?

Jared: That one you're holding. She wrote a number one in the corner.

Thomas: So, what are you going to do about it?

Jared: I don't know. She keeps writing me, but I don't know what to say.

Thomas: Well, why don't you answer her?

Jared: I told you, I don't know what to say.

Thomas: Hey, Jared. You don't even know what she wrote. You can't read it, can you?

Jared:	I can't read her writing.
Thomas:	Jared, she printed these. They're easy to read.
Jared:	For you, Mr. Schoolboy.
Thomas:	For anyone who can read, Jared.
Jared:	(*Grabbing letter back*) Just gimme my letters back and forget it, okay? I can read fine, okay?
Thomas:	No, not okay. Listen, how did you get so far without reading?
Jared:	So far—eighth grade? How far is that? I got passed through sixth and seventh grades because the counselor says it would hurt my self-esteem to be left back.
Thomas:	Doesn't this hurt worse?
Jared:	Not if no one knows.
Thomas:	What'll you do about high school?
Jared:	Probably go into some special program. Don't ruffle your little feathers over it, schoolboy.
Thomas:	Hey, Jared, cut the names. You want to know what the letters say or not?
Jared:	Yeah.
Thomas:	How about I read them to you after school? I won't tell anyone.
Jared:	That's cool. Then I gotta answer them.

Thomas: You can use the computer in the library.
               I'll help.

Jared: Why are you doing this?

Thomas: I'm making a deal. You quit bugging me and
               putting me down, and I'll keep your secret
               and help you.

Jared: That's blackmail.

Thomas: I like to think of it as cooperation. Figure it
               this way—you have nothing to lose and
               everything to gain. If you learn to read,
               you'll be much better off than you are now,
               and I'll be happy.

Jared: Okay, deal. But you tell anyone, and you're a
               dead man, got it?

Thomas: Got it.

Clean Up Your Act

As the scene opens we see a pile of clothing in the middle of the floor. James enters, walks right over the pile as if it isn't there. A chair and table should be on the stage. If there is a stage setting, there can be garbage piled high in the trash, or dishes piled in a sink.

James: Hey, Carl, I'm home. What's for dinner? *(There is no response.* James *throws his books down, moves to sit down, notices clothes on floor.)*

Hey! What're my clothes doing on the floor? Hey, Carl? *(He picks up clothes, then moves them to a chair.)*

Carl: *(Enters)* What is it?

James: Where were you?

Carl: I was studying with the earphones on. What do you want?

James: How come my clothes are all over the floor?

Carl: They're not all over the floor, they're in a pile. Which is not how I found them.

James: Well, put them back in my room.

Carl: No, you put them back—in your closet. Or in drawers.

James: Hey, what is this? I don't have to listen to you. Who appointed you the boss?

Carl: Nobody made me boss, okay? But nobody made me servant, either. I'm tired of cleaning up after you and doing your chores. Which reminds me—you can do the dishes and empty the garbage, too.

James: Hey, I'm serious—knock it off! I don't need you on my back, okay?

Carl: No! Not okay! I am sick and tired of coming home to a mess which I have to clean up because you're too lazy and selfish to do it.

James: Then just leave it alone.

Carl: The only reason I do it is so that Dad won't come home to a filthy house. He has enough on his mind without having to deal with a mess every day. Did you ever think of that? (*He sits down, his face in his hands.*)

James: (*Is silent for a while. Then slowly, he takes one piece of clothing from the pile, folds it neatly, puts it on the table. He continues doing this.*) I'm sorry. You're right—I didn't think about Dad.

Carl: He still looks pretty bad.

James: He seems so lonely and lost without Mom.

Carl: Yeah. That's why I think we have to make things comfortable for him, so he won't feel as if everything is falling apart.

James: I didn't realize I was making such a mess.

	You just did everything, the way mom always did.
Carl:	Yeah, well, every time I did it I got angry. You need to be responsible for your own stuff, okay?
James:	I will. Honest. (*Finishes with clothes*) So— what's for dinner?
Carl:	I don't know—what are you making?

If It Feels Good

Karin: Are you going to Jason's party?

Laura: No.

Karin: How come?

Laura: I don't like his parties.

Karin: How can you say that? They're the best parties in the whole school.

Laura: They're a little too noisy for me. And there's too much going on. You might be smarter not to go.

Karin: What do you mean? That's what makes them exciting.

Laura: I don't need that kind of excitement.

Karin: "That kind of excitement." What's that supposed to mean?

Laura: Come off it, Karin. You know exactly what I'm talking about. Those guys have their own little stash of drugs, and I don't want to be a part of that whole scene.

Karin: Fine, then don't. Just because you're a little scared, that doesn't mean the rest of us can't have a good time.

Laura: And just what is it I'm scared of, Karin?

Karin: Drugs. You act as if one time will kill you.

Laura: No I don't. I act as if drugs are just as dangerous as fire—I don't even want to get burned once. You think you're being so cool, in with the right crowd. But the fact is, you're just another little freshman girl who'll eventually be able to pay for what they're giving you now for free.

Karin: Oh, get a life, Laura.

Laura: I have a life. And I like it just the way it is. If you want to screw yours up, go right ahead.

Karin: I'm not screwing up my life, for cryin' out loud. I'm just having fun.

Laura: Why can't you have fun with friends who like you? Why do you have to go someplace where people don't even know you to have a good time?

Karin: They may not know me now, but they will. And I know all of them, which helps.

Laura: Yes, all the "heads." The head cheerleader, the head jock, the head clown. You want to hang around with the important high school kids. Well, high school's small. Any jerk can be important here.

Karin: Just leave me alone, Laura.

Laura: No problem. And have a nice time at the party. (Karin *exits*)

With all those people there, you'll be more alone than you know.

True Love

∞

A Series of Monologues and Dialogues
About Who and What We Love

True Love I

This character periodically comes on stage. She always appears happy, even at the worst turn of events.

I think Robert likes me. Last Tuesday, when I asked him if he'd done his homework, he told me to shut up. But I think he was just warning me that Mrs. Bradford was watching, and he didn't want to get me in trouble. I just love a protective man!

Today I sat next to Robert on the bus. He told me it bugged him that I was always following him around, and that he wished I would find someone else to bother. That's a really good sign. I mean, Robert is really shy, and yet around me he's able to express his true feelings. That means he really feels safe with me. He probably doesn't even know the depth of his feelings.

Divorce

My mom and dad just got a divorce. It hurts. Now they're arguing about who gets to keep me. I guess that's better than my friend Jason. His parents argued about who *had* to take him. Now he lives with his grandmother.

Anyway, I don't know who to choose. It's difficult. Lately I've been staying at my friend's house. At least I don't have to hear them every day, fighting. My mom cries a lot when she's on the phone with my dad. It's been so hard on me, and they say they love me, but if they do, why are they making my life so miserable?

Why can't they just get married again? They must have loved each other once. They promised to love each other forever. Is that how long forever is . . . just as long as things go well? I love them both, but if they can break a promise to love each other, how do I know they'll always love me? They say they will, but maybe someday they'll want to divorce themselves from me.

Can't they understand that I don't know who to choose? I don't want to choose. And I don't want to be from a divorced family.

I hope when I grow up I don't ever have to get a divorce. I don't want to hurt my children. I don't want to break up anyone else's life.

Inside Out

Callie: What do you think of the new boy in our math class?

Sasha: Gregory? I don't. He's a nothing.

Callie: No he's not. He's sweet. And smart. And he's got beautiful eyes.

Sasha: Yeah—and tennis shoes from K-Mart.

Callie: So? So he's not a Calvin Klein model. Who cares?

Sasha: Please, Callie. He looks like a refugee.

Callie: Maybe he is.
(Sasha *laughs*)

No, really. Maybe he comes from Russia or somewhere, and his parents are really poor.

Sasha: That's right, Callie, romanticize him, so it'll be okay that he dresses like a hick.

Callie: Hey, drop it, okay? I like the guy. And I am sick and tired of worrying about what someone wears or whether they are up on the latest fashion. There is such a thing as nice poor people, y'know.

Sasha: Fine. Why don't you start buying your clothes at Goodwill?

Callie: God you are such a snob!

Sasha: Oh, look who's talking. Miss "I only buy stuff if it's advertised in *Seventeen* or *Elle*."

Callie:	That is not true. But even if it were, that doesn't mean I can't like people who dress differently.
Sasha:	Fine, Callie. Do what you want. Marry the guy for all I care.
Callie:	I haven't even gone out with him yet.
Sasha:	*Yet?* You mean you would? You would actually go out with that dork?
Callie:	Yes, I would. I will. He's going to help me with algebra on Friday, and who knows where it could lead.
Sasha:	Well, have fun with Mr. Refugee. Personally, I think he's just someone who doesn't know how to dress, and you'll be stuck with him once you start to show him any attention.
Callie:	You know, if you dressed most of the guys in our crowd in "K-Mart" clothes, as you call them, they wouldn't be worth looking at or talking to. Jason, on the other hand, is worth looking at and talking to now. Clothes would only make him look better on the outside, but on the inside he's got more than any of the guys we know.
Sasha:	Fine. Just don't expect me to double date if you two go out.
Callie:	Don't worry—you won't be invited.

Mother (or Dad)

Kids today—say they're in love when they're twelve. Ten, even. What the heck do they know about love at that age? They get all that garbage from television.

Ya wanna know what love is? I'll tell you. Love is seeing your kid ride her first bike. Or watching her walk into her kindergarten class while your heart is breaking with pride and fear.

You know you have to let go, but you miss her every second she's away. It's sitting up through the night making sure she's still breathing when she has a high fever. It's praying that she makes the right friends and turns out okay. Love is waiting up till all hours, pretending you're watching television so she won't know you're worried. Love is knowing, in the middle of screaming, that this life means more to you than your own.

So my kid's friend comes to our house the other day, hysterical, crying. Her "boyfriend" broke up with her. The kid's ten for cryin' out loud. And she's howling about how she loves him and now he won't talk to her.

So I try to calm her down, and I say, "Okay, so what's his name?"

"P-P-Paul," she tells me, between sobs.

"What's his last name?"

"I don't knoooooow!" she wails.

Kid's in love, doesn't even know the boy's last name. Gimme a break.

Like I said, kids today don't even know what love is.

Such Devoted Sisters

My sister can be such a brat. She was born four years after me, and I really hated her at first. Well, I didn't really hate her. Deep down, I thought she was a beautiful, tiny miracle. But I was so jealous. She came, and I wasn't the center of attention any more.

My sister probably thought sometimes that she hated me. I mean, I used to lock her out of my room, and tell her not to bug me, and tease her and get her in trouble, and . . . well, you know what I mean. But when she got a good grade on something, she always showed me, not to show off, but so that I would be proud of her. And when she was scared of the dark, or thunder, she'd always crawl in with me.

I know I haven't always been nice to her. Like the time I locked her in the bathroom by putting a chair under the doorknob. Or the time I told this really gross kid that she liked him. But I really do love her. After all the years, through all the silly things I've done to drive her crazy and tell her she isn't wonderful, she still trusts me and loves me.

So that's why, tomorrow, I'm going to the hospital. That's where she's been for a week. But I'm not going to visit her. See, she needs a kidney, and I'm a perfect match. So, because I love her so much, I'm going to give her one of mine. She's my little sister. It's the least I can do.

True Love 2

Today I told Robert I really liked him. He said he didn't like me. It hurt my feelings. I mean, I thought he was sending me signals, but now he denies it. Well, I don't need him. There are plenty of other boys around school. I don't need Robert.

Tony sits next to me in math. He's sooo cute. I think I like him. He usually comes late, and he almost never does his homework, but he's very artistic. I think if I offer him some help in math maybe he'll start to like me, too.

Conceited

I love myself, but my friends say I'm conceited. The nerve!
I mean, what's wrong with loving yourself? You know what
I think? I think they're jealous because I look better, I dress
better, I have a nicer house and a nicer car. I'm rich, and
they're not.

Take Janice, for instance. The other day she wore the same
clothes she'd worn the day before. I mean, really, how
embarrassing! If I had to do that, I just wouldn't go to
school. No wonder she doesn't think much of herself.

I, on the other hand, think I'm very special. I love myself
because I have all the nicest things, and I know how special
I am.

I have to admit that sometimes I worry about the future.
I mean, I have to marry someone who can buy me pretty
things, and have a nice house and car. If I don't, I could end
up being a nobody. Then I might not like myself so much.

My Friend

Monica thinks she's the best. I can't understand her. She treats everyone else like dirt. I'm her friend, and she's even mean to me. Can't she get it that no one likes her?

Just because she's rich doesn't mean that she owns everything. She's so stuck up. No one will say anything to her. The kids hang around her because she has money, but they don't like the way she acts, and they talk about her behind her back.

I'm her friend. I've tried to talk to her, but she won't listen. She seems to think that if someone doesn't like her, then they have a problem.

She always says she loves herself. But if she loves herself so much, how come she needs so much *stuff*? With all she owns, she's still not happy.

So why am I her friend? I guess because I know her. I've known her since kindergarten, and I know that she's really sweet and kind under all that other dumb behavior. And I know that one day, when she wakes up and realizes how she's been acting, she'll need a friend. And I'll be there. That's what friends are for.

Nature Is Love

Isn't it nice to stop and smell the roses? To hug a tree? To lie in the grass after a fresh rain? I love nature. She is rolling hills, and thunderstorms, and rosy sunsets followed by golden sunrises. She is the fish in the oceans, and the oceans themselves, stretching out of sight across the horizon. Nature is the rainforests, nurturing us all with the oxygen they give us as their gift. Nature is the majestic mountains, rising to the high, thin air where clouds float at their peaks.

Nature has produced one imperfection: humans. We destroy Mother Earth and rob her of her resources without paying her back for what we have taken. Yet, no matter how much we destroy her, the Earth loves us back, and keeps trying to give us what we need. Nature is a wild and loving thing. And I love her back.

Tink Loves Me

No matter what happens, I know Tink loves me. She listens to my problems and understands how I feel about everything. She's the only one I feel I can love right now. All my parents do is work. They don't even know—or care—what I'm feeling. They're too busy thinking about themselves and their careers, and their busy social life.

Maybe I should run away. Yeah, that's what I can do. Then maybe they'll think about how I feel, and stay home sometimes. I love them, but at the same time they make me so angry and scared that it's hard to feel loving. I mean, it seems they take more time deciding where to go on vacation than they do on me.

I think I'll go to my grandma's house and talk to her. She loves me enough to listen. I'll take Tink with me. If I don't, who knows if my parents will take care of her. They're so wrapped up in their own lives, they don't have time to think about a little dog. But, as I said, no matter what, I know Tink loves me.

Grandmas and Grandpas Know How to Love Best

Did you ever notice how it's your grandma or grandpa who seems to know just what you need? I'm not talking about stuff, though they certainly can sometimes go a little overboard with that.

I mean, if you're feeling disgusting, they know you might need to talk—but they don't push. Or if you're really happy, they know it might be private, and they let you be happy without trying to find out why you feel good. And they never seem to worry about the little things.

My mom, on the other hand, always wants to find out *exactly* why I'm happier than usual on a particular day, like it's a landmark event or something. And she always wants to make sure I don't eat anything before dinner, or I'll spoil my appetite. But Nanny always has some sliced turkey, and fruit, and lots of cookies, in case I feel like snacking. I never pig out or anything, but it's nice to know it's there.

You know what I think? I think that mothers and fathers are all uptight, because it's their first time doing all this, and they think they have to be perfect, and do what all the books say, or what their parents did. But personally, I think grandparents really know how to love because it's their second time around, and they can love us without all the hassle. And I do have to admit, if I had to put up with dirty diapers, kiddie flu, and back-talk maybe I wouldn't be so thrilled with my kids 24 hours a day either. But grandparents get to just love us, without the details.

Come to think of it, it's a pretty good arrangement. Maybe I'll skip being a parent and just adopt grandkids when I'm older.

True Love 3

Tony likes me! He's been letting me do his homework
every day, and I sit next to him, so when we take quizzes
he can see the answers. I don't think it's so terribly wrong.
After all, you have to help the person you love to succeed.
Don't you?

This afternoon I saw him with one of the cheerleaders. She's
really pretty, but she's not as smart as I am, so I don't think
Tony is really interested in her. He only went to the dance
with her because she asked him, and he didn't want to be
rude. He's really a gentleman.

Secret Love

Anna: Was that Bobby Lyman you were talking to on the bus?

Paul: Yeah.

Anna: What were you guys talking about?

Paul: Stuff.

Anna: Stuff? What stuff? What did he say?

Paul: Nothing special. Why are you so interested, anyway?

Anna: I'm not that interested. I just wondered. (*Long pause*) So what were you guys talking about?

Paul: WHAT IS THE BIG DEAL? We were just talking, okay?

Anna: Did he mention me?

Paul: You? Why would he mention you? (Beat) Oh, I get it!

Anna: What? What d'you get?

Paul: You like him!

Anna: Me? Like Bobby? Are you crazy? You have got to be nuts!

Paul: Then why are you so interested? Huh?

Anna: I'm not. Forget it. Forget I said anything, okay? (*Long pause*) Okay, I like him. A little.

	But if you tell anyone, I'll kill you. Now— *what were you guys talking about?*

Paul: You.

Anna: (*Really excited*) Me? Really? You are kidding. Oh, my gosh! What did he say?

Paul: He said . . . (*Smiles in a teasing way*)

Anna: What? (*Pauses and waits*) What?! (*Impatient, but still waiting.*) WHAT?!

Paul: He said it drives him crazy when you stare at him in math class.

Anna: I don't stare at him. He did not say that.

Paul: Yes, he did. But he also said he thinks you're cute.

Anna: He thinks I'm cute? Ohmigosh! He thinks I'm cute. Ooh! Oh goody!
(*Grabs Paul by the arm*) Now tell me *exactly* what he said. Do not leave out one word! What did he look like when he said it? Ohmigosh! This is incredible!

Paul: (*Trying to get away from her*) Get away from me! Leave me alone! You are so boy crazy! Get out of my face!

Anna: Tell me everything he said. Don't leave out a thing! Ohmigosh, ohmigosh!
(*They exit with Anna following Paul, begging for information, and Paul protesting and trying to get away. They talk over each other as they leave.*)

Chocolate Dreams

At night, when I go to bed, I don't dream of falling in love with movie stars like some people do. Me, I dream of chocolate. I love chocolate in any form. Fudge. Chocolate fudge cake. Brownies . . . well, you get the idea.

Some people are chocoholics. They *have* to have chocolate. Not me. I can walk around for days with a candy bar in my purse and never eat it. Just knowing it's there is comforting. As long as there's other chocolate to eat somewhere.

For Christmas my parents bought me a subscription to *Chocolate* magazine. I read all the recipes. I even try some of them. I have a picture of a German chocolate layer cake inside my locker.

Okay, you can laugh. But the fact is, even though chocolate's not perfect, it will never make fun of me, or leave me alone at a dance, the way Sherman Meller did to my friend Melanie. And chocolate is always pleasant, beautiful to look at, and always available. And as long as there's a 7-11 open, I can get chocolate any time I want.

Now, if Kevin Brown were made of chocolate—that would be perfect!

She Loves Me—I Think

Bobby: Well, what did she say?

Paul: She went nuts, that's what.

Bobby: Nuts bad or nuts good?

Paul: It all depends on how you look at it. I suppose "nuts good." She started carrying on, grabbing me, asking me exactly what you said. I guess she likes you.

Bobby: She does? Cool. Just as long as she doesn't get carried away. I mean, I like her and all, but I don't want her hanging all over me.

Paul: Hey, she's my sister, okay? She's cool. Besides, she doesn't have to hang all over anyone—plenty of guys would love to take her out.

Bobby: Oh yeah? Then how come she didn't go to the last dance at school?

Paul: She was sick.

Bobby: Oh. (*Thinks for a moment*) So, should I ask her out?

Paul: Don't ask me. I'm her brother, for cryin' out loud. Don't ask me if you should ask my sister out.

Bobby: I'm just trying to make sure I don't make a fool of myself.

Paul: Too late.

Bobby:	Funny, Paul. No listen, do you think she'd say yes if I asked her? I mean, she's pretty popular and all.
Paul:	Bobby, just ask her. The worst she can do is say no. Then you won't have to worry about it any more.
Bobby:	Yeah.
Paul:	Just let me give you a word of advice.
Bobby:	Yeah?
Paul:	This is my sister, right? I don't want to hear about your dates, not from you, not from anyone. No blabbing, got it?
Bobby:	What? I don't blab. I might talk over a date with you now and then, but I don't tell stories.
Paul:	Oh yeah? How about your long two-week relationship with Amanda? The whole locker room heard about that. All I'm saying is, I don't want to hear about my sister and your dates, and I don't want anyone else to hear about them. Got it?
Bobby:	Got it. Geez.
Paul:	Ask her out if you want, but just be cool.
Bobby:	Now you've taken half the fun out.
Paul:	Then don't ask her.
Bobby:	Maybe I won't.
Paul:	You're weird, y'know that?

Blue Jeans

This character is a little bit ditzy.

I love my blue jeans. It's weird how someone can feel about just a few yards of denim. But I don't feel myself without them. My mom says I take better care of my jeans than I do of myself. Like, when I wash them I turn them inside out so they won't fade. And I wash them on the gentle cycle. I hang dry them so they won't shrink.

I like my jeans to fit just right. I like them baggy, but they have to fit at the waist and hips. And they have to be blue. I mean, they're not *called* black jeans, right? And blue denim goes with everything, right? I mean, they *are* the miracle color.

Last night I got dressed up to go to my friend's party. I wore this beautiful satin blouse and my new gold earrings and my jeans. My mom says that's not dressed up. But she doesn't understand; blue jeans are the most dressy, undressy, casual, formal clothes you can have.

So, like I said, I love my jeans.

True Love 4

Okay, so Tony was a jerk, and I should have known better. After all, there were plenty of signals, I just didn't want to see them. It's hard sometimes to face the truth.

But I'm learning. For the next few weeks, all I'm going to do is pay attention to schoolwork and my clubs.

And, I think it's time for me to pay attention to me.

Parents

I'm so mad at my parents! I got grounded. Again! Just because I came home a little late last night, I'm grounded for a week.

This is so unfair! My friend Kelly didn't even get in trouble. She is so lucky. Her parents aren't strict at all. Half the time when she comes home late, her parents are asleep. Or they're watching television, and they just tell her to go to bed.

Kelly says I'm the lucky one. She says sometimes she does stuff just to see how much she can get away with before her parents set a limit. So far they never have.

Actually, when I think of it, my mom and dad work really hard to be good parents. I mean, I remember my mom staying up with me when I was sick. I was really little, and I guess I had a high fever. I was dreaming I had a guardian angel, and all of a sudden I opened my eyes, and there was my mom. She was crying. I guess she was really scared for me.

And I guess it's pretty hard, with all that's going on today, to raise your kid, hoping she's okay. My mom never goes to sleep unless I'm home. Last week my class went on a ski trip, y'know? And we got stuck in the snow. I called my mom and told her we were okay, but that I would be really late. I told her not to wait up, but when I got home, she and my dad were both curled up on the couch, trying hard not to fall asleep. No matter how old I am, my mom says I will always be her baby.

My dad sometimes drives me crazy, asking me if I have all my homework done, or trying to talk to me about serious stuff, like, being careful around boys and stuff. I remember when I was in fourth grade, he was worried that I wouldn't get any Valentine's Day cards, so he sent me ten. (*Little laugh*) Ten cards! He went a little overboard, I guess.

Soo . . . what was I saying? Oh yeah, that my parents bug me. (*Small grin*) Well . . . I guess even though they bug me, I really love them. But, most of all, I know, because they work so hard at it, that they love me.

Nobody Loves a Bully

I hate this new school. I knew I would. The kids all hate me. So do the teachers. I hate the stinky food in the cafeteria. I'm miserable.

In my elementary school, I was the biggest kid in my class. I beat up everybody, and everybody was scared of me. It was great. I could go anywhere I wanted, and kids were nice to me, because if they weren't, I'd beat them up.

In this school there are girls a head taller than me. Samantha Ritchie already told me if I so much as looked at her little sister cross-eyed, she'd beat the stuffing out of me. And she is *big*. So I stay away from her little sister. I stay away from everyone. I hate it.

I guess my reputation followed me from my last school. But I've changed. I decided I didn't like hitting people after my cousin Mark got beat up. I mean, I didn't think about what it felt like to get beat up, 'cause I was always the one doing the beating. But he was hurt really bad, and he couldn't go out of the house for a month. So I talked to him a lot, and he explained how only angry people beat people up, and he asked me about why I was so angry.

I never thought about it before, but I was angry a lot. Mostly it was because of Mom leaving. I know she didn't want to leave, but she smoked all the time, and even when the doctors told her she was sick, cigarettes were more important to her than I was. She wouldn't even try to get better for me. Now she's gone, and nobody loves me.

The thing is, nobody even knows me. They think I'm still a bully, but I'm a different person. All I need is a chance. Just one person. Just one.

God Loves Me

At night, when I am all alone, I talk to God. Not pray.
I don't pray. I don't ask for anything. I just talk to him.
Ever since my mom left and went to heaven, I have
conversations with God. I figure, now that she's gone,
God's the only one who loves me.

My foster parents like me. I mean, what's not to like?
I clean the house, cook supper, and help with the babies.
And I get good grades. I don't cause trouble. So of course
they like me.

But they don't love me. Right now, no one loves me. No
one even sees me, really. Except God. God knows I am
here, and he knows I am good. So, no matter what happens,
I'm not really alone, because wherever I am, God will
watch over me and take care of me. And that helps. It helps
to know that God loves me.

Dog Loves Boy

I love my boy. He's so good to me. He lets me sleep with him, and he gives me bits of food when his mom isn't looking. He brushes me and gets rid of my fleas.

(*Looks off to one side*) Now there's a good-looking young lady. My boy would like her.

Where was I? Oh yes—my boy. I would do anything for him. Now, some people might think there's a thin line between loyalty and stupidity. But I think loyalty is honor. We dogs have honor, which is not stupid at all.

And my boy is loyal to me, too. He protects me when I do something bad, like have an accident in the laundry, or simply get too excited and lick his dad's face just before he's going out to work.

(*Looks off again*) H'mm—there's a cute little poodle over there. I could really go for her. And her little girl's not too bad, either. Maybe my boy and I could double.

So—where was I? Oh yeah. My boy.

I love my boy for his kindness. He's so sweet. He won't ever let me stay out in the rain, or make me sleep in my dog house, even on the night I ruined his science project. He told me his teacher would never believe it if he said his dog ate it. I said I would go and tell the teacher I did it, but my boy didn't understand me. But even though he didn't understand my words, he knows. My boy is good. I love my boy.

True Love 5

There's this boy in my science class named Carl. I'd never noticed him before, because he's new in class, and I have been focusing on my work, not on boys. But today he came over and asked me if I have a boyfriend. He smiled at me. He asked me to the dance. It's funny; I wasn't even looking, and someone found me. Wow! Love sure is funny.

Integrating Curriculum

❦

"**D**rama is considered a 'fluff' course," my principal once told me. But she is determined to keep it, because she has seen that through drama students can gain confidence and poise, learn about scientists and artists, think about the condition of the planet, and learn about real communication. Drama is an excellent tool to make the academic curriculum real to students. Here are some of the many ways you can integrate other subjects with drama.

Literature

After students read a book and select a scene they think is important, have them do the following:

1. *Give a short summary of the book up to the chosen scene. Explain what the scene is about.*

2. *Write the scene as a short play, using stage business, props, and costumes when necessary.*

3. *Perform the scene. You may want to tell what happens after the scene, but you may leave your audience in suspense if you like.*

Or, ask students to rewrite and act out a fairy tale, myth, or part of a novel from a different point of view.

Media, History, and Current Events

Students perform "The News As You Wish It Could Be." This gives them the opportunity to look at current events, develop ideas to change the world for the better, and think about the future. It also teaches them the demeanor of newscasting, which is a different form of acting than stage acting. Consider these news items to report on:

> a dinner held in honor of the doctor who found the cure for cancer in 2002,

> a dispute over which people from what professions should be chosen as the next travelers to the new moon colony.

This project allows students to study current events, science, art, or any other subject. In a variation called "The News As It Was," students can present news from a particular day in history, including topics in current events, advertising, fashion, sports, science, and so on. Or, have students pick famous people in history and research their lives. In either case, the students *become* their characters. Students may also choose to give speeches as their characters, trying to persuade or inform the audience about a particular subject. For instance, Marconi might explain how his new invention (the radio) works, or Florence Nightingale might try to convince doctors of the necessity of sanitary conditions in hospitals.

Bibliography

A BOOK FOR TEACHERS OF ACTING

Hagen, Uta. *Respect for Acting*. New York: MacMillan, 1979.

This book contains a wealth of information about the acting profession. It has been around a long time, but is still considered one of the most important handbooks for actors, with many ideas for advanced activities.

Teachers who teach acting should always be able to talk about the profession with authority. This book gives a very broad view of the art and craft of acting.

SCENE BOOKS

A word of advice here: some of the scenes in these books are more appropriate for older students. Still others are better for young middle-school students. Moreover, it is wise to check for language that you feel is inappropriate before giving a scene to students to perform.

Karshner, Roger. *Scenes for Teenagers*. Toluca Lake: Dramaline Publications, 1986.

Kehret, Peg. *Acting Natural*. Colorado Springs: Meriwether Publishing, Ltd. 1991.

Kehret, Peg. *Acting Natural*. Colorado Springs: Meriwether Publishing, Ltd., 1991.

Kehret, Peg. *More Winning Monologs for Young Actors*. Colorado Springs: Meriwether Publishing, Ltd., 1988.

Kehret, Peg. *Winning Monologs for Young Actors*. Colorado Springs: Meriwether Publishing, Ltd., 1986.

Krell-Oishi, Mary. *Scenes That Happen*. Colorado Springs: Meriwether Publishing, Ltd., 1991.

Krell-Oishi, Mary. *More Scenes That Happen*. Colorado Springs: Meriwether Publishing, Ltd., 1994.

Roddy, Ruth Mae. *Scenes for Kids*. Toluca Lake: Dramaline Publications, 1991.

Roddy, Ruth Mae. *Monologs for Kids*. Toluca Lake: Dramaline Publications, 1987.